WIRELESS EXPLOITS AND COUNTERMEASURES

KALI LINUX NETHUNTER, AIRCRACK-NG, KISMET, AND WIRESHARK

4 BOOKS IN 1

BOOK 1
WIRELESS EXPLOITS AND COUNTERMEASURES: A BEGINNER'S GUIDE

BOOK 2
MASTERING KALI LINUX NETHUNTER FOR WIRELESS SECURITY

BOOK 3
AIRCRACK-NG TECHNIQUES: CRACKING WEP/WPA/WPA2 KEYS

BOOK 4
KISMET AND WIRESHARK: ADVANCED WIRELESS NETWORK ANALYSIS

ROB BOTWRIGHT

Published by Rob Botwright
Library of Congress Cataloging-in-Publication Data
ISBN 978-1-83938-650-3
Cover design by Rizzo

Disclaimer

The contents of this book are based on extensive research and the best available historical sources. However, the author and publisher make no claims, promises, or guarantees about the accuracy, completeness, or adequacy of the information contained herein. The information in this book is provided on an "as is" basis, and the author and publisher disclaim any and all liability for any errors, omissions, or inaccuracies in the information or for any actions taken in reliance on such information. The opinions and views expressed in this book are those of the author and do not necessarily reflect the official policy or position of any organization or individual mentioned in this book. Any reference to specific people, places, or events is intended only to provide historical context and is not intended to defame or malign any group, individual, or entity. The information in this book is intended for educational and entertainment purposes only. It is not intended to be a substitute for professional advice or judgment. Readers are encouraged to conduct their own research and to seek professional advice where appropriate. Every effort has been made to obtain necessary permissions and acknowledgments for all images and other copyrighted material used in this book. Any errors or omissions in this regard are unintentional, and the author and publisher will correct them in future editions.

BOOK 1 - WIRELESS EXPLOITS AND COUNTERMEASURES: A BEGINNER'S GUIDE

BOOK 2 - MASTERING KALI LINUX NETHUNTER FOR WIRELESS SECURITY

BOOK 3 - AIRCRACK-NG TECHNIQUES: CRACKING WEP/WPA/WPA2 KEYS

BOOK 4 - KISMET AND WIRESHARK: ADVANCED WIRELESS NETWORK ANALYSIS

Introduction

Welcome to "Wireless Exploits and Countermeasures: Kali Linux NetHunter, Aircrack-ng, Kismet, and Wireshark," a comprehensive book bundle that explores the dynamic and ever-evolving landscape of wireless network security. In a world increasingly connected through wireless technology, the importance of safeguarding our digital assets has never been more critical.

This bundle consists of four distinct volumes, each designed to cater to a range of skill levels, from beginners taking their first steps into the world of wireless security to seasoned professionals seeking advanced insights and techniques.

"Book 1 - Wireless Exploits and Countermeasures: A Beginner's Guide" serves as your gateway to this fascinating realm. Whether you are new to wireless networks or looking to solidify your foundational knowledge, this volume provides a gentle introduction to the fundamental concepts of wireless security. Learn how wireless networks operate, understand the threats they face, and discover essential tools and strategies for securing them.

For those ready to take a deeper dive into the world of mobile security assessments, "Book 2 - Mastering Kali Linux NetHunter for Wireless Security" is your guide. Kali Linux NetHunter, a powerful and specialized platform, is explored in detail. Discover how to set up your NetHunter environment, conduct advanced Wi-Fi scanning, and execute wireless exploits with confidence.

"Book 3 - Aircrack-ng Techniques: Cracking WEP/WPA/WPA2 Keys" is dedicated to the art of breaking Wi-Fi encryption. Aircrack-ng, a versatile suite of tools, is demystified, and readers are equipped with the knowledge and techniques needed to assess wireless network vulnerabilities and strengthen their security.

"Book 4 - Kismet and Wireshark: Advanced Wireless Network Analysis" takes you on a journey into the realm of advanced network analysis with Kismet and Wireshark. Explore passive and active reconnaissance, wireless packet capture, traffic analysis, and the detection and response to wireless attacks. This volume empowers you to conduct in-depth wireless network assessments and troubleshoot complex issues.

Throughout this book bundle, we emphasize the importance of ethical hacking practices and responsible disclosure. Wireless networks are the backbone of modern connectivity, and securing them is a shared responsibility. Whether you are a beginner or an expert, our goal is to equip you with the skills and knowledge needed to protect your networks, devices, and data in an ever-changing digital landscape.

As we embark on this journey through wireless exploits and countermeasures, we invite you to embrace the spirit of exploration, curiosity, and continuous learning. The challenges and opportunities in the world of wireless security are boundless, and with the insights gained from this bundle, you are well-prepared to navigate this exciting and vital field.

Now, let's dive into the depths of wireless network security and arm ourselves with the tools and knowledge needed to secure our digital world.

BOOK 1
WIRELESS EXPLOITS AND COUNTERMEASURES
A BEGINNER'S GUIDE

ROB BOTWRIGHT

Chapter 1: Understanding Wireless Networks

Wireless communication protocols have transformed the way we connect and share information in the modern world. These protocols enable devices to communicate with each other wirelessly, providing convenience and flexibility in our daily lives. From smartphones to Wi-Fi routers, the use of wireless communication has become ubiquitous.

Wireless networks use a variety of protocols to facilitate communication, and understanding these protocols is crucial for anyone interested in the field of wireless security and ethical hacking. In this book, we will explore the intricacies of these protocols and how they play a vital role in both our personal and professional lives.

One of the fundamental aspects of wireless communication is the way data is transmitted over the airwaves. Unlike wired networks, where data travels through physical cables, wireless networks rely on radio waves to transmit information between devices. This wireless transmission introduces unique challenges and vulnerabilities that require careful consideration.

To understand wireless communication protocols better, it's essential to distinguish between different types of wireless networks. Two of the most common are cellular networks and Wi-Fi networks. Cellular networks, such as 4G and 5G, are used for mobile communication, enabling voice calls, text messages, and internet access on smartphones and tablets.

Wi-Fi networks, on the other hand, are typically used for local area networking within homes, businesses, and public spaces. They provide wireless internet access to devices like laptops, smartphones, and smart TVs. Both cellular and Wi-Fi networks rely on specific protocols to function efficiently and securely.

In wireless communication, the protocol refers to a set of rules and conventions that govern how data is transmitted, received, and processed between devices. These protocols ensure that data is delivered accurately and securely, and they dictate how devices should behave when communicating with each other.

One of the most well-known wireless communication protocols is the IEEE 802.11 standard, commonly referred to as Wi-Fi. The IEEE 802.11 standard defines how wireless devices should connect to a network, transmit data, and manage network resources. It encompasses various sub-standards, such as 802.11b, 802.11g, 802.11n, and the more recent 802.11ac and 802.11ax, each offering different speeds and capabilities.

Within the Wi-Fi standard, security is a significant concern. To protect data transmitted over Wi-Fi networks, several encryption and authentication protocols have been developed. The most common encryption protocols used in Wi-Fi networks are WEP (Wired Equivalent Privacy), WPA (Wi-Fi Protected Access), and WPA2. Each of these protocols aims to safeguard data from unauthorized access and interception.

However, as technology advances, so do the methods used by hackers to exploit vulnerabilities in wireless communication. This is where ethical hacking and security assessments come into play. Ethical hackers, also known as penetration testers, use their knowledge of wireless communication protocols and security flaws to identify weaknesses in networks and devices. They then work to secure these vulnerabilities, ultimately helping organizations protect their data and infrastructure.

In the world of ethical hacking, tools like Aircrack-ng play a crucial role. Aircrack-ng is a suite of tools specifically designed for assessing and securing Wi-Fi networks. It includes utilities for capturing data packets, analyzing network traffic, and even attempting to crack WEP and WPA/WPA2 encryption keys. These tools are essential for ethical hackers to test the security of Wi-Fi networks and identify potential weaknesses.

Another valuable tool in the arsenal of ethical hackers is Kismet. Kismet is a wireless network detector, sniffer, and intrusion detection system. It helps identify hidden wireless networks, capture network traffic, and detect unauthorized access points. Ethical hackers use Kismet to perform passive reconnaissance and gain insights into the wireless landscape of a target network.

While Aircrack-ng and Kismet are powerful tools for assessing wireless networks, they should only be used for ethical and legal purposes. Unauthorized or malicious activities can have severe consequences, both legally and ethically. Therefore, it is essential for individuals interested in ethical hacking to obtain proper authorization before conducting any assessments on networks or systems that do not belong to them.

In addition to Wi-Fi networks, cellular networks also require careful consideration in terms of security. The protocols used in cellular networks, such as GSM (Global System for Mobile Communications) and LTE (Long-Term Evolution), play a vital role in ensuring secure communication between mobile devices and cell towers.

One of the challenges in cellular network security is the protection of voice and data transmissions. Encryption protocols like A5/1 and A5/3 are used to secure voice calls and data traffic in GSM and 3G networks. However, as technology evolves, so do the techniques used by attackers to intercept and compromise these communications. Ethical hackers specializing in cellular network security must stay up-to-date with the latest developments in encryption and authentication protocols.

In recent years, the rollout of 5G networks has brought new opportunities and challenges to the world of wireless communication. 5G promises faster speeds, lower latency, and increased connectivity, making it an attractive option for a wide range of applications, from autonomous vehicles to IoT (Internet of Things) devices.

However, the adoption of 5G also introduces new security considerations. As more devices and critical infrastructure rely on 5G networks, the potential impact of security breaches becomes more significant. Ethical hackers will need to adapt their skills and techniques to address the unique challenges posed by 5G, including the protection of network slicing, edge computing, and the increased complexity of the network architecture.

In this book, we will explore the intricacies of wireless communication protocols, from Wi-Fi to cellular and 5G networks. We will delve into the world of ethical hacking and penetration testing, providing insights into the tools and techniques used to assess and secure wireless networks. Whether you are a beginner looking to understand the basics or an experienced professional seeking to expand your knowledge, this book will serve as a valuable resource in your journey to master the field of wireless exploits and countermeasures.

Wireless networks have become an integral part of our daily lives, providing us with the flexibility and convenience of connecting to the internet and other devices without the constraints of physical cables.

These wireless networks use various technologies and protocols to transmit data over the airwaves, allowing us to access information, communicate, and work remotely from virtually anywhere.

One of the most common types of wireless networks is Wi-Fi, which stands for Wireless Fidelity. Wi-Fi networks are prevalent in homes, businesses, coffee shops, airports, and many public spaces.

They offer wireless internet access to a wide range of devices, including laptops, smartphones, tablets, and smart TVs.

Wi-Fi technology operates in the radio frequency (RF) spectrum, typically using the 2.4 GHz and 5 GHz bands, to enable wireless communication between devices and access points.

Another type of wireless network is cellular, which is primarily used for mobile communications. Cellular networks provide voice calls, text messaging, and internet access to mobile devices, including smartphones and feature phones.

Cellular technology relies on a network of cell towers that transmit and receive signals to provide coverage to large geographic areas.

Cellular networks use a variety of technologies and generations, such as 2G, 3G, 4G (LTE), and 5G, each offering different levels of performance and capabilities.

Satellite networks are yet another type of wireless communication system, operating in space to provide coverage to remote and inaccessible regions of the world.

These networks use satellites orbiting the Earth to relay signals between ground stations and satellite dishes installed on user premises.

Satellite communication is commonly used for services like satellite television, global positioning systems (GPS), and remote internet access in rural areas.

Bluetooth is a short-range wireless technology designed for personal area networking, allowing devices like smartphones, laptops, headphones, and speakers to connect wirelessly over short distances.

Bluetooth is commonly used for tasks like transferring files, connecting to wireless peripherals, and streaming audio.

Zigbee and Z-Wave are wireless protocols designed specifically for low-power, low-data-rate applications in smart homes and the Internet of Things (IoT).

These protocols enable smart devices like thermostats, door locks, and sensors to communicate with each other and with centralized controllers.

Mesh networks, a more recent development in wireless technology, have gained popularity in creating resilient and self-healing wireless networks.

In a mesh network, each device can communicate with other nearby devices, forming a dynamic and interconnected network that can adapt to changes in the environment or device availability.

This type of network is useful in scenarios where traditional wireless infrastructure may be impractical or unreliable.

Wireless communication protocols play a vital role in enabling devices to communicate seamlessly and securely over wireless networks.

These protocols define the rules and conventions that devices must follow to establish connections, transmit data, and manage network resources.

The IEEE 802.11 standard, commonly known as Wi-Fi, is a set of protocols that govern wireless local area networking (WLAN).

Wi-Fi protocols define how devices should connect to a network, transmit data, and negotiate network resources.

Within the Wi-Fi standard, there are several sub-standards, such as 802.11b, 802.11g, 802.11n, 802.11ac, and 802.11ax, each offering different speeds and features.

To secure Wi-Fi networks, encryption and authentication protocols like WEP (Wired Equivalent Privacy), WPA (Wi-Fi Protected Access), and WPA2 are used to safeguard data transmission and prevent unauthorized access.

However, as technology evolves, new security challenges arise, and ethical hackers play a crucial role in identifying vulnerabilities and helping organizations protect their networks.

Aircrack-ng is a suite of tools specifically designed for assessing and securing Wi-Fi networks.

Ethical hackers use Aircrack-ng to capture data packets, analyze network traffic, and even attempt to crack WEP and WPA/WPA2 encryption keys.

Kismet is another valuable tool in the arsenal of ethical hackers, used for wireless network detection, sniffing, and intrusion detection.

Kismet helps identify hidden wireless networks, capture network traffic, and detect rogue access points.

The field of ethical hacking involves using these and other tools to assess the security of wireless networks and identify potential weaknesses.

It's crucial to emphasize that ethical hackers must obtain proper authorization before conducting any assessments on networks or systems that do not belong to them.

Unauthorized or malicious activities can have severe consequences, both legally and ethically.

In the world of wireless communication, cellular networks also demand attention when it comes to security.

Protocols like GSM (Global System for Mobile Communications) and LTE (Long-Term Evolution) are used to secure voice calls and data transmissions in cellular networks.

However, as technology evolves, attackers find new ways to intercept and compromise these communications, making it essential for ethical hackers specializing in cellular network security to stay updated with the latest developments in encryption and authentication protocols.

The advent of 5G networks has brought both opportunities and challenges in wireless communication.

5G promises faster speeds, lower latency, and increased connectivity, making it attractive for various applications, including autonomous vehicles and the Internet of Things (IoT).

However, the adoption of 5G introduces new security considerations, given the increased complexity of the network architecture and the potential impact of security breaches.

Ethical hackers will need to adapt their skills and techniques to address these unique challenges.

In this book, we delve into the intricacies of wireless communication protocols, from Wi-Fi to cellular and 5G networks.

We explore the world of ethical hacking and penetration testing, providing insights into the tools and techniques used to assess and secure wireless networks.

Whether you are a beginner seeking to understand the basics or an experienced professional looking to expand your knowledge, this book serves as a valuable resource in your journey to master the field of wireless exploits and countermeasures.

Chapter 2: Wireless Security Fundamentals

Common wireless threats pose significant challenges to the security and privacy of wireless networks in our increasingly connected world. These threats exploit vulnerabilities in wireless communication protocols and network configurations, potentially leading to data breaches, unauthorized access, and disruptions in network services.

One of the most prevalent wireless threats is eavesdropping, where unauthorized individuals intercept and monitor wireless communications without the knowledge or consent of the parties involved. Eavesdropping can result in the exposure of sensitive information, such as passwords, credit card numbers, and personal messages.

Another common wireless threat is unauthorized access, which occurs when an attacker gains entry to a wireless network without proper authentication. Attackers often exploit weak or default passwords, open network configurations, or flaws in authentication protocols to access network resources.

Rogue access points represent a significant threat to wireless networks, as they are unauthorized wireless access points that mimic legitimate network infrastructure. These rogue access points can capture sensitive data or redirect users to malicious websites, compromising network security.

Wireless denial-of-service (DoS) attacks disrupt the normal functioning of a wireless network by overwhelming it with a flood of traffic or malicious requests. These attacks can result in network downtime, rendering it inaccessible to legitimate users.

Another wireless threat is the injection of malicious code into network traffic, which can lead to the compromise of connected devices or the interception of sensitive data. Attackers may use techniques like packet injection or malware distribution to carry out these attacks.

Man-in-the-middle (MITM) attacks are a common wireless threat where attackers intercept and potentially alter communications between two parties without their knowledge. This type of attack can lead to the theft of sensitive information or the injection of malicious code into network traffic.

Brute-force attacks are attempts to guess or crack passwords by systematically trying every possible combination until the correct one is found. Attackers often use brute-force attacks to gain access to wireless networks or online accounts protected by weak or easily guessable passwords.

Password attacks also include dictionary attacks, where attackers use predefined word lists to guess passwords. These word lists may include common phrases, words, and variations, making it easier for attackers to find the right password.

WEP (Wired Equivalent Privacy) is an older and less secure wireless encryption protocol that is susceptible to attacks, such as packet sniffing and dictionary attacks. Attackers can exploit vulnerabilities in WEP to gain unauthorized access to a network.

WPA (Wi-Fi Protected Access) and its predecessor, WPA2, have been widely adopted to enhance wireless security.

However, these protocols are still vulnerable to attacks, including password cracking and brute-force attacks.

WPS (Wi-Fi Protected Setup) is a feature designed to simplify the process of connecting devices to a Wi-Fi network. However, it has known vulnerabilities that can be exploited by attackers to gain access to the network.

SSID (Service Set Identifier) broadcasting is a common practice in wireless networks where the network name is broadcast openly. Attackers can exploit this by using rogue access points with the same SSID to trick users into connecting to malicious networks.

Spoofing attacks involve impersonating legitimate network devices or access points to deceive users into connecting to the attacker's network. These attacks can lead to data theft or unauthorized access.

EAP (Extensible Authentication Protocol) is a commonly used authentication framework in wireless networks. However, some EAP methods are vulnerable to attacks that can compromise user credentials and network security.

War driving is a practice where attackers drive around to locate and identify wireless networks, potentially to exploit vulnerabilities or gain unauthorized access.

MAC address spoofing allows attackers to impersonate authorized devices by changing their MAC (Media Access Control) addresses. This can be used to bypass MAC filtering security measures.

To mitigate these common wireless threats, it is essential to implement robust security measures and best practices. These include using strong encryption protocols like WPA3, regularly updating firmware and security patches, disabling unnecessary network services, implementing strong access controls, and conducting security assessments and audits.

Wireless security is an ongoing process that requires continuous monitoring and adaptation to address evolving threats and vulnerabilities in the dynamic landscape of wireless communication.

Principles of wireless security are essential for protecting the confidentiality, integrity, and availability of data transmitted over wireless networks.

Wireless networks have become pervasive in our daily lives, connecting everything from smartphones and laptops to smart appliances and IoT devices.

However, the convenience of wireless communication also introduces unique security challenges that must be addressed to prevent unauthorized access and data breaches.

One fundamental principle of wireless security is encryption, which involves encoding data to make it unreadable to unauthorized parties.

Encryption ensures that even if data packets are intercepted, they remain unintelligible without the encryption key.

Modern wireless networks use strong encryption protocols like WPA3 to protect data in transit.

Authentication is another key principle of wireless security, as it verifies the identity of devices and users before granting access to the network.

Effective authentication mechanisms ensure that only authorized devices and individuals can connect to the network.

Access controls play a vital role in limiting network access to authorized users and devices.

Network administrators can define access policies that specify who can connect to the network, what resources they can access, and the level of permissions granted.

Implementing strong access controls helps prevent unauthorized devices from joining the network.

Regularly updating firmware and software is crucial for maintaining the security of wireless devices and access points.

Manufacturers release updates and patches to address vulnerabilities and enhance security features.

Failing to update devices can leave them susceptible to known exploits.

Network segmentation is a security principle that involves dividing a network into smaller, isolated segments.

Segmentation enhances security by limiting the scope of potential breaches.

If one segment is compromised, it does not necessarily lead to the compromise of the entire network.

Wireless Intrusion Detection Systems (WIDS) and Wireless Intrusion Prevention Systems (WIPS) are essential tools for monitoring wireless networks.

These systems detect and respond to suspicious activities and unauthorized access attempts.

WIDS and WIPS help identify and mitigate security threats promptly.

Physical security measures protect the physical components of wireless networks, such as routers, access points, and antennas.

Securing these components prevents unauthorized tampering or theft.

Password policies and practices are fundamental to wireless security.

Requiring strong, unique passwords for network access and regularly changing default passwords can prevent unauthorized entry.

Education and awareness are critical principles of wireless security.

Users should be educated about the risks and security best practices for using wireless networks.

Phishing attacks and social engineering are common tactics used to trick users into divulging sensitive information.

Raising awareness helps individuals recognize and avoid these threats.

Regular security audits and assessments are essential to evaluate the effectiveness of security measures.

Conducting penetration tests and vulnerability assessments helps identify weaknesses in the network's security posture.

Wireless security policies and procedures provide a framework for implementing security measures consistently.

Organizations should have well-documented policies that address aspects such as access control, encryption, and incident response.

A robust incident response plan is essential for mitigating the impact of security incidents.

It outlines the steps to take when a security breach is detected, including notification, containment, and recovery efforts.

Intrusion detection and prevention systems play a crucial role in incident response.

These systems can automatically detect and respond to security breaches.

Encryption keys must be managed securely to maintain the confidentiality of data. Keys should be generated using strong algorithms and stored in a secure manner. Regularly rotating encryption keys enhances security by limiting the exposure of a single key.

Public Wi-Fi networks are a common target for attackers. Users should exercise caution when connecting to public Wi-Fi hotspots, avoiding sensitive transactions and using virtual private networks (VPNs) for added security. Endpoint security is critical in wireless networks.

Endpoint devices like laptops and smartphones should have up-to-date security software to protect against malware and other threats. Wireless security is a shared responsibility.

Users, network administrators, and device manufacturers all play a role in maintaining a secure wireless environment. Security awareness training helps users understand the importance of security measures and the potential consequences of security lapses.

Multi-factor authentication (MFA) is an effective way to enhance authentication security.

MFA requires users to provide multiple forms of identification before gaining access to a network or device.

Wireless networks should be regularly monitored for suspicious activities and anomalies.

Anomalies in network traffic or device behavior can indicate security breaches.

Monitoring allows for timely responses to security incidents.

Wireless security standards and best practices continue to evolve as new threats emerge.

Organizations should stay informed about the latest developments in wireless security and adapt their security measures accordingly.

Security awareness and compliance with security policies are essential for maintaining a secure wireless environment.

Regularly updating and patching devices and access points is vital to address vulnerabilities promptly.

Ultimately, wireless security is an ongoing effort that requires vigilance and a commitment to staying ahead of evolving threats.

Chapter 3: Basic Tools for Network Scanning

In the realm of cybersecurity, network scanning serves as a foundational activity for understanding the vulnerabilities and security posture of computer networks. Network scanning involves the systematic exploration of a network to identify open ports, running services, and potential vulnerabilities. This process provides valuable insights into the network's configuration and potential weaknesses that could be exploited by malicious actors.

Network scanning tools and techniques have evolved significantly over the years, becoming essential components of both offensive and defensive cybersecurity strategies. These tools empower security professionals, administrators, and ethical hackers to assess the security of networks, identify potential weaknesses, and ultimately enhance overall network security.

The importance of network scanning cannot be overstated in today's interconnected world. With countless devices, systems, and services connected to the internet, organizations and individuals must regularly scan their networks to maintain a strong defense against cyber threats. Network scanning allows for proactive identification and remediation of vulnerabilities, reducing the likelihood of successful cyberattacks.

Network scanning can take various forms, depending on the goals and objectives of the scan. One of the most common types of network scans is the port scan. Port scanning involves probing a target network to discover which ports are open and what services or applications are running on those ports. This information is crucial for understanding the attack surface of a network.

Another essential aspect of network scanning is vulnerability scanning. Vulnerability scanners are specialized tools designed to identify known vulnerabilities within networked devices and software. These scanners leverage databases of known vulnerabilities and their associated patches to detect weaknesses that could be exploited by attackers.

Network mapping is another valuable outcome of network scanning. Network maps provide an overview of the network's architecture, including the relationships between devices and how they are connected. These maps help administrators visualize the network's structure, aiding in network management and security assessment.

Intrusion detection systems (IDS) and intrusion prevention systems (IPS) often rely on network scanning techniques to monitor network traffic and detect suspicious or malicious activities. These systems can automatically respond to identified threats by blocking or alerting network administrators, helping to safeguard the network in real-time.

Network scanning is not limited to internal networks; it extends to external network assessments as well. Organizations frequently conduct external scans to assess the security of their public-facing assets, such as web servers and mail servers. These scans help identify vulnerabilities that may be exploited by external attackers. Understanding the legality and ethics of network scanning is essential. Unauthorized scanning of networks or systems that do not belong to you is illegal and unethical.

Ethical hacking and security professionals always seek proper authorization before conducting scans. Unauthorized scanning can lead to legal repercussions and damage trust within the cybersecurity community.

In addition to the legality and ethics of network scanning, it's crucial to consider the impact of scanning on network performance. Intensive or aggressive scans can generate significant traffic and potentially disrupt network operations. Network administrators must carefully plan and execute scans to minimize disruption.

As technology evolves, so do the challenges and opportunities in network scanning. The growth of cloud computing, the proliferation of IoT devices, and the adoption of software-defined networks (SDN) have expanded the attack surface and complexity of modern networks. Network scanning tools and techniques must adapt to these changes to remain effective in identifying vulnerabilities and weaknesses.

In the chapters that follow, we will delve deeper into the world of network scanning, exploring various tools, techniques, and best practices for conducting scans ethically and effectively. Whether you are a network administrator looking to secure your organization's infrastructure or an ethical hacker seeking to assess and improve network security, this book aims to equip you with the knowledge and skills needed to navigate the ever-changing landscape of network scanning.

Essential scanning techniques are the foundation of effective network reconnaissance and vulnerability assessment. These techniques provide security professionals and ethical hackers with the means to identify open ports, discover active services, and detect potential vulnerabilities in target networks and systems. By mastering these techniques, individuals can enhance their ability to assess and improve network security.

Port scanning is one of the fundamental scanning techniques used to identify open ports on a target system. Port scanners send a series of network packets to a range of port numbers to determine which ports are open and accepting connections. Understanding the state of open ports is crucial for identifying potential entry points for attackers.

A common tool for port scanning is Nmap (Network Mapper), which is highly versatile and widely used in the cybersecurity community. Nmap can perform various scanning types, such as TCP, UDP, and SYN scans, allowing users to tailor their scans to specific needs. By analyzing Nmap scan results, security professionals can gain valuable insights into a network's configuration and potential vulnerabilities.

Service enumeration is closely related to port scanning and involves identifying the specific services and applications running on open ports. Once open ports are discovered, service enumeration techniques aim to determine the nature and version of the services running on those ports. This information helps security professionals assess the potential security risks associated with each service.

Banner grabbing is a service enumeration technique that involves retrieving information about a service or application's banner or banner-like response. Banners often contain details about the service version, which can be compared to known vulnerabilities to assess potential risks. Tools like Telnet or specialized banner-grabbing scripts can be used for this purpose.

Operating system (OS) fingerprinting is another essential technique that helps identify the underlying operating system of a target system. OS fingerprinting relies on patterns in network responses to determine the likely OS running on the target. By knowing the OS, security professionals can tailor their scanning and attack strategies accordingly.

One widely used tool for OS fingerprinting is the open-source tool called OS fingerprinting, such as Xprobe and pOf, can also assist in identifying the target OS.

Ping sweeps are scanning techniques used to identify live hosts within a network range. Ping sweeps send ICMP (Internet Control Message Protocol) echo requests to a range of IP addresses to determine which hosts are responsive. Identifying live hosts is a crucial step in preparing for further reconnaissance and vulnerability assessments.

Ping sweeps can be conducted using tools like Nmap or specialized scripts that automate the process. It's important to note that some networks may have ICMP filtering or rate-limiting in place, making ping sweeps less reliable.

UDP scanning is a specialized scanning technique used to identify open UDP ports on a target system. Unlike TCP ports, which have well-defined states, UDP ports may not always provide clear responses. UDP scanning involves sending UDP packets to various port numbers and analyzing the responses to determine which ports are open. Tools like Nmap offer UDP scanning capabilities.

In addition to traditional scanning techniques, stealth and evasion techniques are also essential for ethical hackers and security professionals. These techniques aim to minimize the footprint of scans and reduce the likelihood of detection by intrusion detection systems (IDS) or network administrators.

Fragmentation and decoy techniques are examples of evasion techniques that can be employed during scanning. Fragmentation involves splitting packets into smaller fragments to evade network security mechanisms. Decoy techniques involve sending packets to multiple hosts simultaneously to make it challenging for defenders to identify the true source of the scan.

Scanning techniques also extend to web applications and services. Web application scanning involves assessing the security of web-based applications, including websites and web services. Tools like Burp Suite and OWASP ZAP (Zed Attack Proxy) are commonly used for web application scanning. These tools help identify vulnerabilities such as SQL injection, cross-site scripting (XSS), and insecure authentication mechanisms.

Wireless network scanning is a specialized area of scanning that focuses on assessing the security of wireless networks. Tools like Aircrack-ng and Kismet are used to identify open Wi-Fi networks, capture network traffic, and detect rogue access points. Wireless scanning is essential for securing wireless networks and detecting potential threats.

Intrusion detection and prevention systems (IDS/IPS) play a critical role in network security by monitoring network traffic for suspicious or malicious activity. IDS systems use signature-based and anomaly-based detection techniques to identify potential threats. Understanding how IDS/IPS systems operate is crucial for network defenders and ethical hackers alike.

In the world of ethical hacking, understanding scanning techniques and tools is essential for assessing and improving the security of networks and systems. However, it's important to emphasize that ethical hacking should always be conducted with proper authorization and within the boundaries of applicable laws and regulations. Unauthorized scanning or testing of networks and systems can have legal and ethical consequences.

In the following chapters, we will explore these essential scanning techniques in greater detail, providing insights into their practical applications and real-world scenarios. Whether you are a network administrator seeking to secure your organization's infrastructure or an ethical hacker looking to assess and enhance network security, this book aims to equip you with the knowledge and skills needed to excel in the field of network reconnaissance and vulnerability assessment.

Chapter 4: Exploring Wi-Fi Encryption

Wireless networks have revolutionized the way we connect to the internet and communicate, but they also introduced new challenges in terms of security. In the early days of wireless networking, one of the most widely used encryption protocols was WEP, short for Wired Equivalent Privacy. WEP was developed as a security measure to protect wireless communications by encrypting data as it was transmitted over the airwaves. However, as technology advanced, it became apparent that WEP had significant vulnerabilities that rendered it ineffective at providing robust security.

One of the primary weaknesses of WEP encryption is its reliance on a static and easily guessable encryption key. WEP uses a shared secret key to encrypt and decrypt data transmitted between devices on a wireless network. This key, known as the WEP key or passphrase, is used to both encrypt and decrypt data. The problem with WEP keys is that they are typically short and composed of easily predictable patterns, making them vulnerable to brute-force and dictionary attacks.

WEP encryption uses a stream cipher called RC4 (Rivest Cipher 4) to protect data. RC4 generates a keystream based on the shared WEP key, which is then XORed with the plaintext data to produce the ciphertext. While RC4 itself is not inherently flawed, the way WEP uses it makes the encryption weak. The keystream generated by RC4 is not unique for each packet but is reused across multiple packets. This reuse of the keystream allows attackers to predict and recover portions of the keystream, making it easier to crack the encryption.

Another critical vulnerability of WEP encryption is related to the initialization vector (IV) used in the encryption process. The IV is a 24-bit value that is combined with the WEP key to generate the keystream. Since the IV is relatively short, it means that after a certain number of packets, the same IV value will be reused. This repetition of IVs provides attackers with additional patterns to exploit, further weakening the encryption.

In practice, attackers can collect a sufficient number of encrypted packets, analyze the patterns in the ciphertext, and recover the WEP key using various techniques. One commonly used attack against WEP is the IV collision attack, where an attacker captures packets until collisions in IV values occur. These collisions reveal information about the keystream, making it easier to decrypt subsequent packets.

Another weakness of WEP encryption is the lack of data integrity protection. WEP focuses solely on confidentiality by encrypting the data, but it does not provide mechanisms to ensure the integrity of the data being transmitted. This means that attackers can modify the content of packets without detection, potentially leading to data tampering or injection of malicious content.

The combination of these vulnerabilities made WEP encryption highly susceptible to exploitation. As a result, it did not take long for security researchers and hackers to develop tools and techniques for cracking WEP-protected networks. The availability of software like Aircrack-ng made it relatively straightforward for attackers to target WEP networks and gain unauthorized access.

In response to the widespread recognition of WEP's weaknesses, the Wi-Fi Alliance introduced more secure encryption protocols, such as WPA (Wi-Fi Protected Access) and its successor, WPA2. These newer protocols addressed many of the vulnerabilities found in WEP and introduced stronger encryption mechanisms, including the use of the Advanced Encryption Standard (AES). WPA and WPA2 also improved the management of keys, making it more challenging for attackers to crack the encryption.

Despite the well-documented vulnerabilities of WEP encryption, some older devices and legacy systems may still rely on it for compatibility reasons. However, using WEP in modern wireless networks is strongly discouraged, as it offers minimal security and leaves networks exposed to various attacks. Network administrators and individuals should consider upgrading to more secure encryption protocols like WPA3, which provide robust protection against contemporary threats.

In summary, WEP encryption, once a popular choice for securing wireless networks, is now widely regarded as insecure due to its numerous vulnerabilities. Weaknesses in the WEP key management, reliance on a predictable keystream, and the lack of data integrity protection make WEP encryption ineffective at providing meaningful security. As technology evolves and threats become more sophisticated, it is essential for organizations and individuals to adopt modern and secure encryption protocols to safeguard their wireless communications effectively.

Wireless networks have become an integral part of our daily lives, providing us with the flexibility and convenience of connecting to the internet and other devices without the constraints of physical cables. However, the widespread adoption of wireless technology also brought new security challenges, prompting the development of more robust encryption protocols like WPA (Wi-Fi Protected Access) and WPA2.

WPA and WPA2 were introduced to address the vulnerabilities and weaknesses of the earlier WEP (Wired Equivalent Privacy) encryption protocol. These newer encryption standards significantly improved the security of wireless networks, making them more resistant to various types of attacks.

One of the key improvements introduced by WPA and WPA2 was the use of stronger encryption algorithms. WEP used the RC4 stream cipher, which was vulnerable to attacks that could reveal the encryption key. In contrast, WPA and WPA2 employ the Advanced Encryption Standard (AES), a symmetric-key encryption algorithm recognized for its strength and security.

AES encryption provides robust data protection by using a strong encryption key to scramble data before it is transmitted over the wireless network. The use of AES significantly enhances the confidentiality of data, making it extremely difficult for attackers to decrypt intercepted traffic without knowing the encryption key.

Another critical security enhancement introduced by WPA and WPA2 is the implementation of the 4-way handshake for authentication. The 4-way handshake is a secure exchange of messages between a client device and an access point, which enables both parties to establish a unique encryption key for the session. This dynamic key exchange mechanism prevents attackers from easily capturing and decrypting network traffic.

WPA and WPA2 also introduced the use of a more extensive range of authentication methods, including Pre-Shared Keys (PSKs) and the Extensible Authentication Protocol (EAP). PSKs are commonly used in home and small office networks, where users enter a passphrase to access the network. EAP, on the other hand, offers more advanced and flexible authentication options suitable for enterprise environments.

In addition to stronger encryption and authentication mechanisms, WPA and WPA2 introduced the concept of Temporal Key Integrity Protocol (TKIP) and Counter Mode with Cipher Block Chaining Message Authentication Code Protocol (CCMP). TKIP was initially introduced in WPA to provide improved security over WEP while maintaining compatibility with older hardware. CCMP, on the other hand, became the recommended encryption protocol for WPA2, offering superior security.

One of the advantages of WPA and WPA2 is their backward compatibility with older devices and hardware. This backward compatibility allows users to upgrade their network security without immediately replacing all their wireless devices. However, it's essential to note that older devices may not fully benefit from the enhanced security features of WPA2.

To further enhance security, WPA2 introduced the use of robust security networks (RSNs) and the introduction of the Pairwise Master Key (PMK). RSNs define a set of security features and requirements that must be met by devices to establish secure connections. The PMK is a secret key shared between a client and an access point, used to derive encryption keys dynamically during the 4-way handshake.

Despite the significant improvements in security, WPA2 is not entirely immune to attacks. One notable vulnerability is the WPA2 KRACK (Key Reinstallation Attack) vulnerability, which affects the 4-way handshake process. Attackers can exploit this vulnerability to reinstall encryption keys and potentially decrypt traffic.

To mitigate the risks associated with the KRACK vulnerability and other emerging threats, the Wi-Fi Alliance introduced WPA3 as the latest wireless security standard. WPA3 enhances security by introducing stronger encryption, more robust authentication mechanisms, and protection against brute-force attacks on weak passwords.

In summary, WPA and WPA2 encryption standards represent significant advancements in wireless network security compared to their predecessor, WEP. These standards employ AES encryption, dynamic key exchange mechanisms, and a variety of authentication methods to provide robust data protection. However, users should remain vigilant and consider upgrading to the latest WPA3 standard to ensure they are protected against evolving threats and vulnerabilities.

Chapter 5: Securing Your Own Wi-Fi Network

Creating a strong Wi-Fi password is a crucial step in securing your wireless network against unauthorized access and potential threats. A weak or easily guessable password can make your network vulnerable to intruders who may exploit your internet connection, access sensitive data, or engage in malicious activities.

A strong Wi-Fi password should be a combination of various elements, making it difficult for attackers to guess or crack. One fundamental principle for creating a strong password is to make it long. Longer passwords are generally more secure as they provide more combinations for attackers to guess.

Aim for a minimum password length of at least 12 characters, and consider using even longer passwords if possible. Longer passwords are often more secure than shorter ones, as they require a significantly larger number of guesses to crack.

Another essential element of a strong Wi-Fi password is complexity. A complex password includes a mix of different character types, such as uppercase letters, lowercase letters, numbers, and special symbols. This diversity makes it more challenging for attackers to guess or crack the password using automated tools.

Avoid using easily guessable information in your password, such as common words, phrases, or easily accessible personal information like names, birthdays, or dictionary words. Attackers often use dictionary attacks or brute-force methods to guess passwords, and using common words or phrases makes their job much easier.

Consider using a passphrase instead of a single word or a combination of unrelated characters. A passphrase is a longer sequence of words or a sentence that is easier to remember and can be highly secure if well-chosen. Make sure your passphrase is unique and not easily guessable.

While complexity is essential, it's also crucial to strike a balance between complexity and memorability. If your password is too complex and challenging to remember, you might be tempted to write it down or store it in an insecure manner, which can compromise security.

Avoid using easily guessable patterns or sequences in your password, such as "123456," "password," or "qwerty." These are among the most common passwords and are the first ones attackers try when attempting to breach a network.

Consider using a passphrase or creating a memorable phrase with variations, substitutions, and character replacements to add complexity. For example, "I love hiking in the mountains!" can be transformed into a strong passphrase like "1L0veH!k!ng@theM0unt@1n$!".

Use a different Wi-Fi password than the one you use for other accounts, such as email, social media, or online banking. Reusing passwords across multiple accounts can be risky, as a breach of one account could potentially compromise others.

Regularly update your Wi-Fi password to enhance security. Changing your password periodically can help protect your network, especially if you suspect that it may have been compromised. It's a good practice to change your password at least once a year or whenever you believe there is a potential security threat.

Avoid using default passwords provided by your router manufacturer. Default passwords are often well-known and published online, making it easy for attackers to gain access to routers with unchanged default settings.

Consider enabling additional security features on your wireless router, such as MAC address filtering, which restricts network access to devices with specific MAC addresses, or disabling remote administration to prevent unauthorized changes to your router's settings.

When sharing your Wi-Fi network with others, provide them with a guest network or a separate SSID with its own strong password. This way, guests can access the internet without gaining access to your primary network and its connected devices.

Regularly review the devices connected to your network to ensure that only authorized devices are accessing it. Most modern routers provide a list of connected devices in their settings, allowing you to monitor network activity.

Keep your Wi-Fi password confidential and only share it with trusted individuals. Avoid sharing it with strangers or on public forums, as doing so can increase the risk of unauthorized access.

In summary, creating a strong Wi-Fi password is a critical step in securing your wireless network and protecting your data from potential threats. A strong password combines length, complexity, and memorability while avoiding common patterns and easily guessable information. By following these guidelines and periodically updating your password, you can enhance the security of your wireless network and reduce the risk of unauthorized access.

Enabling network encryption is a fundamental aspect of modern cybersecurity, as it plays a crucial role in protecting sensitive data and communications from unauthorized access and eavesdropping. Network encryption involves the use of cryptographic techniques to secure data as it is transmitted over a network, ensuring that only authorized parties can access and decipher the information.

The need for network encryption has become increasingly evident as the volume of digital data transmission has grown exponentially. In an interconnected world where information travels across the internet and various networks, ensuring the confidentiality and integrity of data has become paramount.

One of the primary purposes of network encryption is to safeguard data from interception by unauthorized entities. Without encryption, data packets traveling over a network can be intercepted and read by malicious actors or eavesdroppers. Network encryption prevents this by transforming the data into a format that is indecipherable without the proper decryption key.

Two fundamental encryption methods are commonly used to protect network data: symmetric encryption and asymmetric encryption. Symmetric encryption involves the use of a single shared secret key that is used both to encrypt and decrypt data. This key must be kept secret and shared only between authorized parties. Symmetric encryption is typically faster and more efficient but requires a secure method for key distribution.

Asymmetric encryption, on the other hand, uses a pair of public and private keys. The public key is freely distributed and can be used to encrypt data, while the private key is kept secret and is used to decrypt the data. Asymmetric encryption provides a higher level of security for key exchange, as the private key is never shared. However, it is computationally more intensive and slower than symmetric encryption.

Secure Sockets Layer (SSL) and its successor, Transport Layer Security (TLS), are widely used protocols that implement network encryption to protect data exchanged between web browsers and web servers. SSL and TLS use asymmetric encryption to establish a secure connection between a client and a server, after which symmetric encryption is often used for the actual data transfer.

The process of enabling network encryption typically begins with the generation and distribution of encryption keys. In symmetric encryption, a single shared key is generated and securely exchanged between the communicating parties. For asymmetric encryption, a public-private key pair is generated for each entity, and the public keys are distributed widely.

Once encryption keys are established, data can be encrypted before transmission and decrypted upon arrival at its destination. This process ensures that even if an attacker intercepts the data packets, they cannot decipher the information without access to the encryption keys.

Virtual Private Networks (VPNs) are a common implementation of network encryption, allowing users to create secure and encrypted connections over the public internet. VPNs use various encryption protocols and tunneling techniques to protect data as it traverses the internet, ensuring that sensitive information remains confidential.

Implementing network encryption can occur at various levels of the network stack, including the application layer, transport layer, and network layer. At the application layer, encryption can be applied selectively to specific data, such as email contents or files. At the transport layer, protocols like SSL/TLS provide end-to-end encryption for data transmitted between two parties. At the network layer, technologies like IPsec (Internet Protocol Security) can encrypt data at the packet level to protect entire communications sessions.

One of the challenges in implementing network encryption is managing encryption keys effectively. Key management involves the generation, distribution, storage, rotation, and disposal of encryption keys. Proper key management practices are essential to ensure the ongoing security of encrypted communications.

Another consideration is the potential impact of encryption on network performance. Encryption and decryption processes consume computational resources, and the additional overhead can introduce latency and reduce network throughput. Therefore, organizations must carefully evaluate the trade-offs between security and performance when implementing network encryption.

The choice of encryption algorithms also plays a crucial role in network security. Strong encryption algorithms provide a high level of security, but they must be kept up to date to resist advances in cryptographic attacks. Older or deprecated algorithms may be vulnerable to attacks and should be avoided.

In summary, enabling network encryption is a critical component of modern cybersecurity, safeguarding data and communications from interception and unauthorized access. Encryption methods like symmetric and asymmetric encryption, along with protocols such as SSL/TLS and IPsec, provide robust security for networks and data transmissions. However, effective key management and careful consideration of performance implications are essential to maximize the benefits of network encryption while maintaining network performance and security.

Chapter 6: Detecting Rogue Access Points

Identifying rogue access points (APs) is a critical aspect of network security, as these unauthorized devices can pose significant threats to the integrity and confidentiality of your network. Rogue APs are typically wireless access points that have been set up without proper authorization within an organization's network, often by employees or malicious actors seeking to gain unauthorized access.

Rogue APs can introduce a range of security risks, including unauthorized access to sensitive data, exposure to external attackers, and the potential for data breaches. It's essential to have mechanisms in place to identify and mitigate these rogue devices effectively.

One common method for identifying rogue APs is through active scanning and monitoring of the wireless network environment. This involves regularly scanning for and identifying any access points that are not part of the authorized network infrastructure. Network administrators use specialized tools and software to perform these scans, checking for rogue APs that may be broadcasting in the vicinity.

Another approach to identifying rogue APs is through passive monitoring of the wireless spectrum. Passive monitoring involves listening to wireless traffic and identifying any access points that are not part of the authorized network. This method is less intrusive and can help detect rogue APs even if they are not actively transmitting data.

Wireless intrusion detection systems (WIDS) and wireless intrusion prevention systems (WIPS) are specialized solutions designed to identify and mitigate rogue APs and other wireless threats. These systems continuously monitor the wireless network environment, detect unauthorized devices, and take actions to mitigate the risks they pose.

One technique used by WIDS and WIPS solutions is signature-based detection, where the systems compare the characteristics of detected APs against known patterns of rogue AP behavior. If a detected AP matches a known rogue AP profile, the system can trigger alerts or take predefined actions to block or isolate the rogue device.

Behavioral analysis is another method employed by WIDS and WIPS solutions to identify rogue APs. These systems monitor the behavior of devices on the network and look for deviations from expected patterns. For example, a device suddenly appearing and broadcasting an open network may be flagged as a potential rogue AP.

Another approach to identifying rogue APs is to leverage the information provided by clients' wireless devices. By analyzing the information broadcast by wireless clients, such as the SSID and BSSID (Basic Service Set Identifier), administrators can detect anomalies that may indicate the presence of rogue APs.

A common strategy for rogue AP identification is to maintain a comprehensive inventory of authorized access points within the organization. This inventory includes details such as MAC addresses, SSIDs, and physical locations. When monitoring the network, any access point not on the authorized list can be flagged as a potential rogue.

Continuous monitoring and regular network scans are essential for promptly identifying rogue APs. Rogue APs can appear at any time, and their presence may change over time. Therefore, it's crucial to have automated and real-time monitoring systems in place to detect and respond to rogue APs quickly.

Once a rogue AP is identified, it's important to take immediate action to mitigate the security risks it poses. Depending on the organization's policies and the severity of the threat, actions can range from alerting administrators and isolating the rogue AP to physically locating and removing the unauthorized device.

Wireless security policies should also be enforced to prevent the unauthorized installation of rogue APs in the first place. These policies should clearly outline the steps for requesting and authorizing new wireless access points, as well as the consequences of violating these policies.

Physical security measures can play a role in rogue AP prevention by restricting physical access to network infrastructure. Access points should be installed in secure locations, and physical security controls should be in place to prevent unauthorized personnel from connecting unauthorized devices to the network.

User education and awareness are essential components of rogue AP prevention. Employees should be educated about the risks associated with rogue APs and instructed on the proper procedures for requesting and setting up wireless access points within the organization.

In summary, identifying rogue access points is a critical aspect of network security that requires proactive monitoring, specialized tools, and robust policies and procedures. Rogue APs can introduce significant security risks, and organizations must have mechanisms in place to detect and respond to these unauthorized devices promptly. By implementing a combination of technical controls, policies, and user education, organizations can enhance their ability to protect their wireless networks from rogue AP threats.

Mitigating rogue access point (AP) threats is a crucial aspect of network security, as these unauthorized devices can introduce significant risks to an organization's network infrastructure and data. Rogue APs can potentially provide attackers with an entry point into the network, enabling them to intercept sensitive information, launch attacks, or compromise network security.

To effectively mitigate rogue AP threats, organizations need to implement a multi-faceted approach that combines technical controls, policies, and user awareness.

One of the primary methods for mitigating rogue AP threats is through continuous network monitoring and scanning. Network administrators should regularly scan the wireless spectrum to detect any unauthorized access points that may have been deployed within the organization's premises. These scans can identify rogue APs by analyzing their MAC addresses, SSIDs, signal strength, and other characteristics.

Advanced wireless intrusion detection systems (WIDS) and wireless intrusion prevention systems (WIPS) can play a significant role in identifying and mitigating rogue APs. These systems continuously monitor the wireless network environment and can automatically detect unauthorized devices, classify them as rogue APs, and take predefined actions to mitigate the threat.

Automated actions taken by WIDS and WIPS systems may include disabling the rogue AP, isolating it from the network, or alerting network administrators for further investigation. The ability to respond quickly to rogue APs is essential for minimizing the potential impact of security breaches.

Using intrusion detection and prevention systems can significantly enhance an organization's ability to detect and respond to rogue APs effectively. However, it's important to configure these systems correctly and regularly update their signatures and rules to adapt to new threats.

An essential aspect of mitigating rogue AP threats is implementing strict access control measures on the organization's wired and wireless networks. By restricting network access to authorized devices only, organizations can reduce the chances of rogue APs connecting to the network. Access control lists (ACLs) and network segmentation can help enforce these restrictions.

Network segmentation, in particular, can isolate critical network segments from less secure areas, limiting the potential impact of rogue APs in the event of a breach. By isolating sensitive data and systems, organizations can prevent unauthorized access and data leakage.

Education and user awareness are essential components of rogue AP mitigation. Employees should be educated about the risks associated with rogue APs and the potential consequences of deploying unauthorized wireless access points. Clear policies and procedures for requesting and setting up new wireless access points should be communicated to all staff members.

Employees should be encouraged to report any suspicious or unauthorized wireless devices they encounter within the organization. A reporting mechanism should be established to allow users to easily report rogue APs to the IT department for investigation and mitigation.

To prevent the inadvertent deployment of rogue APs, organizations should maintain a centralized inventory of all authorized access points. This inventory should include details such as MAC addresses, SSIDs, and physical locations of access points. Any access point not on the authorized list should be investigated and either approved or removed.

Physical security measures can also contribute to rogue AP mitigation. Access to network infrastructure should be restricted to authorized personnel only, and physical controls should be in place to prevent unauthorized individuals from connecting unauthorized devices to the network.

Regularly updating and patching network devices and access points is crucial for mitigating rogue AP threats. Outdated firmware or software on access points can introduce vulnerabilities that attackers can exploit. By keeping access points up to date, organizations can reduce the potential attack surface.

In cases where a rogue AP is detected, it's important to have an incident response plan in place. The plan should outline the steps to take when a rogue AP is identified, including isolating the device, conducting a thorough investigation to determine its origin, and assessing the impact on network security.

Legal considerations also come into play when mitigating rogue AP threats. Organizations should be aware of local and national regulations governing the use of wireless communication devices and the interception of wireless signals. Compliance with these regulations is essential to avoid legal consequences.

In summary, mitigating rogue access point threats is a complex but essential aspect of network security. Organizations need to combine technical controls, policies, user education, and vigilant monitoring to detect and respond to rogue APs effectively. By taking a proactive approach to rogue AP mitigation, organizations can reduce the risks associated with unauthorized wireless devices and protect their network infrastructure and data.

Chapter 7: Password Cracking Techniques

Dictionary attacks are a common method employed by attackers to gain unauthorized access to user accounts and systems. In a dictionary attack, the attacker uses a predefined list of words, phrases, or commonly used passwords to guess the authentication credentials of a target account or system. The goal of a dictionary attack is to find a matching username and password pair, allowing the attacker to log in and potentially compromise the account or system. Dictionary attacks are often used against login pages, email accounts, and network services that require authentication. One reason dictionary attacks are popular among attackers is that they are relatively simple to execute and can be automated using software tools. Attackers compile dictionaries of potential passwords by using common words, phrases, and patterns, often derived from leaked password databases or publicly available sources. These dictionaries can contain thousands or even millions of entries, making it possible to test a large number of credentials quickly. Dictionary attacks are particularly effective when users choose weak or easily guessable passwords. Weak passwords often consist of common words, phrases, or patterns that can be found in standard dictionaries. For example, passwords like "password123," "admin," or "qwerty" are highly susceptible to dictionary attacks because they are included in most dictionaries used by attackers. To protect against dictionary attacks, organizations and individuals should enforce strong password policies. Strong passwords are typically long, complex, and include a combination of uppercase letters, lowercase letters, numbers, and special characters. By requiring users to create strong passwords, organizations can significantly reduce the risk of successful dictionary attacks. Another defense against dictionary attacks is the use of account lockout policies. Account lockout policies lock user accounts after a certain number of unsuccessful login attempts. This prevents attackers from repeatedly guessing passwords, as they will be locked out of the account after a specified number of failed attempts. However, account lockout policies should be implemented carefully to avoid inconveniencing legitimate users. Attackers may attempt to bypass account lockout policies by using distributed dictionary attacks, where multiple attackers attempt to log in from different IP addresses to avoid triggering account lockouts. To defend against distributed dictionary attacks, organizations can implement rate limiting or intrusion detection systems to detect and block suspicious login attempts. Additionally, multi-factor authentication (MFA) is an effective defense against dictionary attacks. MFA requires users to provide two or more forms of authentication before gaining access to an account or system. Even if an attacker guesses the correct password, they would still need to provide the additional authentication factors, such as a one-time code generated by a mobile app or a hardware token. This significantly increases the complexity of successfully compromising an account. In addition to protecting individual accounts, organizations should also secure their network services and systems against dictionary attacks. For example, they can implement intrusion detection and prevention systems (IDPS) to monitor and block dictionary attacks against network services. Web application firewalls (WAFs) can also help protect against dictionary attacks by filtering out suspicious login attempts and traffic. Password policies should be enforced not only for user accounts but also for privileged accounts and administrative access. Attackers often target administrative accounts with dictionary attacks, as compromising them can provide full control over a system or network. Privileged accounts should have strong, unique passwords and should not share passwords with regular user accounts. Regularly auditing and reviewing password policies and access controls is essential for maintaining security against dictionary attacks. Organizations should also educate their employees about the importance of choosing strong passwords and the risks associated with weak passwords. Training programs can help users understand the significance of password security and encourage them to create and maintain strong passwords. Password managers can be valuable tools for both individuals and organizations in the fight against dictionary attacks. Password managers can generate strong, random passwords for each account and store them securely, reducing the risk of using weak or easily guessable passwords. They can also help users keep track of numerous complex passwords, making it easier to maintain good password hygiene. To further protect against dictionary attacks, organizations can monitor and analyze login attempts and traffic patterns for suspicious activities. Anomalies, such as a sudden increase in login attempts or unusual login locations, can be indicators of dictionary attacks in progress. By continuously monitoring for these signs, organizations can detect and respond to dictionary attacks in real-time, minimizing potential damage. In summary, dictionary attacks are a common and effective method used by attackers to gain unauthorized access to user accounts and systems. Protecting against dictionary attacks requires a combination of strong password policies, account lockout mechanisms, multi-factor authentication, and user education. Organizations should also implement security measures, such as intrusion detection systems and web application firewalls, to defend against dictionary attacks targeting network services. Regular monitoring and analysis of login attempts and traffic patterns can help organizations detect and respond to dictionary attacks promptly. By taking these proactive steps, individuals and organizations can strengthen their defenses against dictionary attacks and enhance overall security. Brute-force attacks are a common and aggressive method used by cybercriminals to gain unauthorized access to computer systems, accounts, and encrypted data. In a brute-force attack, the attacker systematically tries all possible combinations of passwords or encryption keys until the correct one is found. These attacks are characterized by their persistence and exhaustive nature, as they involve testing a vast number of possibilities until success is achieved. Brute-force attacks can target various types of systems and services, including login pages, email accounts, encrypted files, and Wi-Fi networks. One of the primary weaknesses exploited by brute-force attacks is weak or easily guessable passwords. Users who choose simple passwords like "password," "123456," or their own names are at high risk of falling victim to brute-force attacks. To defend against brute-force attacks, organizations and individuals should implement strong password policies. Strong passwords are typically long, complex, and include a combination of uppercase letters, lowercase letters, numbers, and special characters. The complexity of strong passwords makes them resistant to brute-force attacks, as the number of possible combinations becomes extremely large. Brute-force attacks can be time-consuming and resource-intensive, especially when targeting strong passwords. Attackers may require significant computational power and time to guess a complex password. One technique used to reduce the time required for brute-force attacks is the use of password dictionaries. Password dictionaries are lists of commonly used passwords, words from dictionaries, and known phrases. Attackers often use these dictionaries to focus their brute-force attacks on likely password candidates. To protect against dictionary-based brute-force attacks, organizations should enforce password policies that prohibit the use of easily guessable passwords found in dictionaries. Additionally, users should be educated about the importance of creating unique, strong passwords that cannot be easily cracked by attackers. Another defense against brute-force attacks is the implementation of account lockout policies. Account lockout policies temporarily lock user accounts after a specified number of consecutive failed login attempts. This prevents attackers from repeatedly guessing passwords and slows down the brute-force process. However, organizations should carefully configure account lockout policies to avoid inconveniencing legitimate users. Attackers may attempt to bypass account lockout policies by using multiple IP addresses or proxies to distribute login attempts. To mitigate this, organizations can implement rate limiting and intrusion detection systems to detect and block suspicious login activity. Multi-factor authentication (MFA) is a highly effective defense against brute-force attacks. MFA requires users to provide two or more forms of authentication before gaining access to an account or system. Even if an attacker guesses the correct password, they would still need to provide the additional authentication factors, such as a one-time code generated by a mobile app or a fingerprint scan. This significantly increases the complexity of successfully compromising an account. Brute-force attacks can also target encrypted data, such as files or network traffic. In these cases, attackers attempt to guess the encryption key used to protect the data. The effectiveness of brute-force attacks against encryption depends on the strength of the encryption algorithm and the length of the encryption key. Strong encryption algorithms with long keys can make brute-force attacks computationally infeasible, even for attackers with substantial resources. To protect against brute-force attacks on encrypted data, organizations should use robust encryption algorithms and maintain the confidentiality of encryption keys. Regularly updating and patching systems and software is crucial for defending against brute-force attacks. Outdated systems or software may have known vulnerabilities that attackers can exploit to gain unauthorized access. By keeping systems up to date, organizations can reduce the potential attack surface. When brute-force attacks are detected or suspected, organizations should have an incident response plan in place. The plan should outline the steps to take when a brute-force attack is identified, including isolating affected systems, investigating the source of the attack, and mitigating the threat. Legal considerations are also relevant when dealing with brute-force attacks. Organizations must be aware of local and national regulations governing computer and network security, as well as the consequences of unauthorized access attempts. In summary, brute-force attacks are a persistent and aggressive method used by attackers to gain unauthorized access to systems, accounts, and encrypted data. Strong password policies, account lockout mechanisms, multi-factor authentication, and user education are effective defenses against brute-force attacks. Organizations should also monitor and analyze login attempts and traffic patterns to detect and respond to brute-force attacks in real-time. By implementing proactive security measures and following best practices, individuals and organizations can strengthen their defenses against brute-force attacks and enhance overall security.

Chapter 8: Network Traffic Analysis

Packet capture, also known as packet sniffing or network traffic analysis, is a fundamental technique in the field of networking and cybersecurity. It involves the interception and analysis of data packets as they flow across a computer network. Packet capture provides valuable insights into network behavior, troubleshooting network issues, and identifying security threats. To perform packet capture, you need a network interface in promiscuous mode, which allows it to capture all network traffic, not just the traffic intended for the host. Tools like Wireshark, Tcpdump, and Tshark are commonly used for packet capture and analysis. Packet capture can be used for various purposes, including network troubleshooting, performance analysis, and security monitoring. Network administrators often use packet capture to diagnose network problems, such as slow performance or connectivity issues. By analyzing captured packets, they can identify the source of the problem and take appropriate corrective actions. Packet capture is also crucial for monitoring network performance and optimizing network resources. It allows organizations to analyze traffic patterns, identify bottlenecks, and make informed decisions to improve network efficiency. In the realm of cybersecurity, packet capture is a powerful tool for detecting and investigating security incidents. Security professionals use packet capture to monitor network traffic for signs of malicious activity, such as intrusion attempts or data exfiltration. By capturing and analyzing packets, they can uncover the tactics and techniques used by attackers. Packet capture can reveal unauthorized access attempts, suspicious communication patterns, and data breaches. Packet capture operates at the data link layer and captures packets at the lowest level of the network stack. It captures packets as they traverse the network interface, before they are processed by higher-level protocols or applications. This low-level capture allows for detailed analysis of packet headers and payload content. Packet capture can be performed on various types of networks, including wired and wireless networks. For wired networks, packet capture typically involves connecting to a network switch or hub and configuring the capturing device to monitor the desired traffic. On wireless networks, capturing packets may require specialized hardware or software to capture over-the-air traffic. When performing packet capture, it's essential to consider the potential impact on network performance. Capturing and analyzing a high volume of network traffic can consume significant resources, potentially affecting network performance. To minimize this impact, it's advisable to capture only the relevant traffic and use filtering to narrow down the scope of captured packets. Packet capture filters allow you to specify criteria for selecting packets of interest, such as source or destination IP addresses, port numbers, or specific protocols. By applying filters, you can focus on capturing the packets that are most relevant to your analysis or investigation. Packet capture also plays a crucial role in network forensics, which involves investigating and analyzing network-related incidents. Network forensics professionals rely on packet capture to reconstruct network activities and identify the sequence of events during an incident. They use captured packets to piece together the timeline of an attack or security breach. Packet capture is often integrated into intrusion detection systems (IDS) and intrusion prevention systems (IPS) to monitor network traffic continuously. When suspicious activity is detected, these systems can trigger packet capture to capture additional information for analysis. Packet capture files can become quite large, depending on the volume of network traffic and the duration of the capture. Storage requirements should be considered when setting up packet capture solutions. Packet capture files are typically saved in a format like PCAP (Packet Capture), which is widely supported by analysis tools. Once packets are captured, they can be analyzed using various network analysis tools and protocols. Wireshark, for example, is a popular and powerful open-source packet analysis tool that allows for in-depth inspection and interpretation of captured packets. Wireshark provides a user-friendly interface for browsing and filtering packets, as well as advanced features for protocol analysis and decryption. Analyzing packet captures may require expertise in networking and cybersecurity, as well as a deep understanding of network protocols and behavior. Packet analysis can reveal valuable information, such as IP addresses, port numbers, protocol usage, and communication patterns. It can also provide insights into the content of network traffic, including application data and payloads. Security analysts often use packet analysis to identify indicators of compromise (IoC) and potential security threats. By examining packet payloads, they may discover malicious code or unauthorized access attempts. Packet capture can be particularly useful in incident response, allowing organizations to investigate security incidents and develop countermeasures. For example, during a malware outbreak, packet capture can help security teams identify infected hosts and trace the origin of malicious files or traffic. Additionally, packet capture can aid in compliance and regulatory requirements by providing a record of network activities. Organizations subject to data protection laws or industry regulations may use packet capture to demonstrate compliance and maintain audit trails. In summary, packet capture is a foundational technique in networking and cybersecurity that enables the interception and analysis of network traffic. It serves a variety of purposes, including network troubleshooting, performance analysis, and security monitoring. Packet capture is a powerful tool for detecting and investigating security incidents, identifying network anomalies, and optimizing network resources. Security professionals and network administrators rely on packet capture to gain insights into network behavior and respond effectively to network-related challenges and threats.

Analyzing network traffic is a critical aspect of network management, security, and optimization. It involves the examination and interpretation of data packets as they traverse a computer network. By analyzing network traffic, organizations can gain valuable insights into their network's performance, identify security threats, and troubleshoot connectivity issues. Network traffic analysis plays a crucial role in maintaining the integrity, availability, and performance of modern computer networks. Network administrators use traffic analysis tools and techniques to monitor, capture, and analyze the flow of data packets within their network. These tools enable them to understand how data is transmitted, identify patterns of communication, and pinpoint any irregularities or anomalies. One of the primary purposes of analyzing network traffic is performance monitoring. Network administrators use traffic analysis to assess the overall health and efficiency of their network infrastructure. By examining traffic patterns and data flow, they can identify congestion points, bandwidth bottlenecks, and latency issues. Performance monitoring allows organizations to optimize network resources, ensure a smooth user experience, and deliver services more efficiently. In addition to performance monitoring, network traffic analysis plays a crucial role in network troubleshooting. When users experience connectivity problems or application issues, administrators can use traffic analysis to pinpoint the source of the problem. Analyzing network traffic helps them identify network devices, protocols, or services that may be causing disruptions. This information is invaluable for diagnosing and resolving network-related problems promptly. Security is another critical area where network traffic analysis is instrumental. Security professionals use traffic analysis to detect and investigate security incidents, such as cyberattacks, malware infections, and unauthorized access attempts. By scrutinizing network traffic, they can uncover signs of malicious activity, identify vulnerabilities, and respond to threats in a timely manner. Network traffic analysis can reveal indicators of compromise (IoC) and help organizations enhance their cybersecurity posture. To analyze network traffic effectively, organizations deploy various tools and techniques. Packet capture tools like

Wireshark, Tcpdump, and Snort allow network administrators to capture and inspect individual data packets in real-time or from saved packet capture files. These tools provide detailed information about packet headers, payload content, source and destination addresses, and protocols used. Packet capture tools are essential for deep packet inspection (DPI) and protocol analysis. Flow-based analysis tools like NetFlow, IPFIX, and sFlow focus on collecting and analyzing flow records that summarize network traffic between devices. These records contain information such as source and destination IP addresses, ports, protocol types, and packet counts. Flow analysis is particularly useful for understanding network traffic patterns, detecting anomalies, and optimizing network performance. Additionally, flow data is less resource-intensive to collect and analyze than full packet captures. Traffic analysis tools may also include intrusion detection systems (IDS) and intrusion prevention systems (IPS) that monitor network traffic for signs of malicious activity. IDS and IPS tools use predefined signatures and anomaly detection techniques to identify potential security threats. When suspicious traffic is detected, these tools can trigger alerts or take automated actions to mitigate threats. Security information and event management (SIEM) systems are another category of traffic analysis tools. SIEM solutions collect and correlate data from various sources, including network traffic logs, to provide a holistic view of an organization's security posture. SIEM platforms enable security analysts to detect, investigate, and respond to security incidents effectively. Analyzing network traffic for security purposes often involves threat intelligence feeds and behavioral analysis to identify advanced threats. One of the fundamental aspects of network traffic analysis is the ability to filter and aggregate data to focus on specific areas of interest. Filters allow analysts to narrow down the scope of traffic analysis by specifying criteria such as IP addresses, port numbers, protocol types, and time intervals. By applying filters, analysts can isolate and examine specific subsets of network traffic. Aggregation, on the other hand, involves summarizing large volumes of data into more manageable forms, such as charts, graphs, or reports. Aggregated data can help identify trends, anomalies, or significant events within the network. Network traffic analysis tools often provide visualization capabilities, allowing analysts to represent data in a more understandable and actionable format. Effective network traffic analysis requires a combination of technical skills and domain expertise. Analyzing network traffic demands a deep understanding of network protocols, communication patterns, and common network behaviors. It also requires familiarity with the specific tools and techniques used for traffic analysis. Security analysts, in particular, need to stay updated on emerging threats and attack vectors to effectively identify and respond to security incidents. Machine learning and artificial intelligence (AI) are playing an increasingly important role in network traffic analysis. These technologies can automate the detection of anomalies and potential threats by learning from historical network traffic data. Machine learning models can help identify patterns of behavior that deviate from the norm, making it easier to spot malicious activity. As network environments become more complex and dynamic, machine learning and AI-driven traffic analysis tools are becoming indispensable for threat detection and prevention. Network traffic analysis is not limited to on-premises networks. With the proliferation of cloud computing and remote work, organizations must extend their traffic analysis capabilities to cover cloud-based services and remote user connections. This requires the integration of cloud-native traffic analysis tools and the monitoring of virtualized network environments. In summary, analyzing network traffic is a fundamental practice in network management, security, and optimization. Network traffic analysis tools and techniques provide valuable insights into network performance, troubleshooting, and security. By examining data packets and flow records, organizations can enhance their network efficiency, detect and resolve issues, and protect against security threats. As technology evolves, machine learning and AI are becoming increasingly important for automated traffic analysis, especially in complex and dynamic network environments.

Chapter 9: Wireless Intrusion Detection

Wireless networks have become an integral part of modern communication and connectivity. With the proliferation of wireless technology, organizations and individuals can enjoy the benefits of mobility and flexibility. However, the convenience of wireless networks also introduces security challenges and risks. Wireless networks are susceptible to a wide range of security threats, including unauthorized access, data interception, and network intrusion. To address these challenges and protect wireless networks, Wireless Intrusion Detection Systems (WIDS) have emerged as a vital component of network security. WIDS are specialized security systems designed to monitor, detect, and respond to security incidents within wireless networks. They play a crucial role in safeguarding the integrity and confidentiality of wireless communication. WIDS operates by continuously analyzing network traffic and identifying abnormal or suspicious behavior. These systems employ various detection techniques and algorithms to detect security threats and potential intrusions. WIDS can monitor both 802.11 (Wi-Fi) and non-Wi-Fi wireless networks, making them versatile tools for securing different types of wireless environments. The primary goal of WIDS is to provide real-time visibility into wireless network activity and proactively identify security breaches. By detecting and alerting on security incidents, WIDS helps organizations respond promptly to threats and minimize potential damage. WIDS can be deployed in various wireless network environments, including enterprise networks, public Wi-Fi hotspots, and industrial wireless networks. They are particularly valuable in environments where the security of wireless communication is paramount, such as healthcare, finance, and government sectors. WIDS can operate using different deployment models, depending on the specific security requirements and network architecture. One common deployment model is sensor-based, where WIDS sensors are strategically placed throughout the wireless network to monitor traffic and detect intrusions. Another model is network-based, where WIDS is integrated into the existing network infrastructure, allowing it to analyze traffic at key points within the network. Hybrid deployments, combining sensor-based and network-based approaches, are also common and offer a balanced approach to wireless security. WIDS can perform various detection functions, including signature-based detection and anomaly-based detection. Signature-based detection relies on predefined patterns or signatures of known attacks to identify and alert on security threats. It is effective at detecting known and well-documented attack patterns but may miss zero-day attacks or new, previously unknown threats. Anomaly-based detection, on the other hand, focuses on identifying deviations from established network baselines. It looks for unusual or suspicious behavior that may indicate a security breach. Anomaly-based detection is particularly useful for detecting previously unseen attacks but may generate false positives if not properly tuned. WIDS also often includes behavioral analysis, which examines patterns of behavior over time to identify subtle and evolving threats. To provide effective security, WIDS relies on up-to-date threat intelligence and signature databases. These databases contain information about known threats, attack vectors, and vulnerabilities. Regular updates are essential to ensure that WIDS can identify the latest security threats and vulnerabilities. WIDS can provide several essential security capabilities, including rogue AP detection, intrusion detection, and wireless traffic analysis. Rogue AP detection is a critical function of WIDS, as rogue access points can introduce significant security risks. WIDS sensors continuously scan for wireless access points that are not part of the authorized network. When a rogue AP is detected, WIDS can trigger alerts and take predefined actions, such as isolating the rogue AP or disabling it. Intrusion detection is another core capability of WIDS. It monitors network traffic for signs of malicious activity, including unauthorized access attempts, abnormal behavior, and attack patterns. When an intrusion is detected, WIDS generates alerts, allowing network administrators to respond promptly and investigate the incident. Wireless traffic analysis is essential for understanding the composition of network traffic and identifying potential security threats. WIDS can analyze the type of traffic, devices connected, and the applications or services in use. This analysis helps organizations gain visibility into their wireless network and detect any unusual or unauthorized activity. In addition to detection and monitoring, WIDS can provide valuable reporting and analysis capabilities. These capabilities enable organizations to review historical data, assess network security posture, and generate compliance reports. WIDS can also integrate with Security Information and Event Management (SIEM) systems to provide a centralized view of security events across the entire network. To effectively deploy and manage WIDS, organizations must consider several factors. First, it's crucial to define the scope and objectives of WIDS deployment. Organizations should identify the critical assets, locations, and wireless devices that require protection. Understanding the specific security requirements and compliance obligations is essential in tailoring WIDS deployment accordingly. Next, organizations should carefully plan the placement of WIDS sensors or integration points within the network. The placement should consider factors such as network topology, wireless coverage, and traffic patterns. Ensuring adequate sensor coverage is essential for comprehensive monitoring and threat detection. Regular maintenance and updates of WIDS components, including sensors and databases, are critical to maintaining effective security. Organizations should establish clear incident response procedures and workflows for handling alerts generated by WIDS. Response plans should define roles and responsibilities, escalation procedures, and actions to take in the event of a security incident. Employee training and awareness programs are essential to ensure that staff members are familiar with WIDS capabilities and understand their role in network security. Regular testing and validation of WIDS deployment are essential to assess its effectiveness. Penetration testing and security assessments can help identify vulnerabilities and weaknesses that need to be addressed. In summary, Wireless Intrusion Detection Systems (WIDS) are indispensable tools for securing wireless networks. They provide continuous monitoring, detection, and response to security threats within wireless environments. WIDS play a crucial role in protecting sensitive data, maintaining network integrity, and ensuring compliance with security standards. Effective deployment and management of WIDS require careful planning, maintenance, and employee training to achieve optimal security outcomes. Deploying a Wireless Intrusion Detection System (WIDS) is a crucial step in enhancing the security of a wireless network. A well-planned deployment ensures that the WIDS effectively monitors network traffic, detects security threats, and provides valuable insights into the network's integrity. Before deploying a WIDS, it's essential to define clear objectives and understand the specific security requirements of your organization. Consider the critical assets, locations, and wireless devices that need protection. Determine the scope of the deployment, whether it covers the entire organization, specific areas, or critical access points. Identifying the goals and scope helps tailor the WIDS deployment to meet your organization's unique needs. The next step in deploying a WIDS is to plan the placement of sensors or integration points within the network. Sensor placement is critical for comprehensive monitoring and threat detection. Consider the physical layout of your wireless network, including the location of access points, network infrastructure, and areas with high wireless traffic. Strategically position WIDS sensors to cover areas where unauthorized access or suspicious activity is most likely to occur. Coverage should include key entry and exit points, sensitive areas, and critical infrastructure. Sensor placement also needs to account for wireless coverage patterns and potential obstacles that may affect signal propagation. In larger deployments, organizations may use a combination of sensor types, including dedicated hardware sensors and software-based sensors integrated into existing network infrastructure. Hybrid deployments that combine sensor-based and network-based approaches offer a balanced approach to wireless security. Ensure that sensors are distributed evenly to provide adequate coverage and eliminate blind spots. Proper sensor placement allows the WIDS to capture network traffic effectively and detect any anomalies or security threats. Once sensors are deployed, they should be configured to monitor the appropriate channels, frequencies, and wireless standards used in the network. Configuration settings may vary depending on the manufacturer and model of the WIDS solution. Ensure that sensors are synchronized with the network's time settings to maintain accurate event timestamps. Consider tuning the sensitivity and detection thresholds of the sensors to minimize false positives and maximize the accuracy of threat detection. Regularly review and update sensor configurations to adapt to changes in the network environment or emerging threats. Integration with other security systems and network infrastructure components is a critical aspect of WIDS deployment. WIDS should seamlessly work with existing security tools, such as firewalls, intrusion prevention systems (IPS), and Security Information and Event Management (SIEM) systems. Integration allows for coordinated incident response and centralized monitoring of security events. WIDS can provide valuable threat intelligence to SIEM systems, enabling organizations to correlate events across the entire network. When deploying WIDS, it's essential to establish clear incident response procedures and workflows. Define roles and responsibilities for incident responders, and establish escalation procedures for handling security alerts. Incident response plans should outline the actions to take when WIDS detects unauthorized access, rogue access points, or other security incidents. Training and awareness programs for employees and security personnel are crucial to ensure that staff members understand WIDS capabilities and their role in network security. Employees should be familiar with incident response procedures and know how to report suspicious activity. Regular training and tabletop exercises can help organizations prepare for security incidents and improve response times. Maintaining WIDS components is an ongoing responsibility in WIDS deployment. Regularly update and patch the sensors and databases to ensure that the WIDS can identify the latest security threats and vulnerabilities. Monitor the health and performance of sensors to ensure that they are operating correctly. Conduct regular audits and assessments of the WIDS deployment to identify and address any weaknesses or areas for improvement. Testing and validation of the WIDS deployment are essential to assess its effectiveness. Penetration testing and security assessments can help identify vulnerabilities and weaknesses that need to be addressed. Periodic security audits can verify that the WIDS is meeting its objectives and providing adequate protection. Review logs and reports generated by the WIDS to identify trends and potential areas of concern. Regularly analyze security events and incidents to understand the evolving threat landscape and adapt your security strategy accordingly. In summary, deploying a Wireless Intrusion Detection System (WIDS) is a critical step in enhancing the security of wireless networks. A well-planned deployment involves defining objectives, planning sensor placement, configuring sensors, integrating with existing security systems, and establishing incident response procedures. Maintenance and ongoing monitoring are essential to ensure the effectiveness of the WIDS in detecting and responding to security threats. Regular testing and validation help organizations identify vulnerabilities and adapt their security strategy to evolving threats. A successful WIDS deployment plays a vital role in protecting sensitive data, maintaining network integrity, and ensuring compliance with security standards.

Chapter 10: Ethical Hacking Best Practices

Responsible disclosure is a fundamental ethical practice in the field of cybersecurity. It is the process by which security researchers, ethical hackers, or concerned individuals report security vulnerabilities or weaknesses they discover to the organizations or vendors responsible for the affected software, hardware, or systems. The objective of responsible disclosure is to alert the responsible party to the vulnerability so that they can take appropriate action to fix it, thereby enhancing the overall security posture. Responsible disclosure is characterized by transparency, collaboration, and adherence to a set of established principles. One of the primary principles of responsible disclosure is the disclosure of vulnerabilities directly to the organization or vendor responsible for the affected product or system. This direct communication ensures that the responsible party is made aware of the issue and can begin the process of addressing it. Security researchers and ethical hackers typically reach out to the organization's security team or through established security contact channels. Publicly disclosing a vulnerability before the organization has had a chance to address it can put users and systems at risk and is generally considered irresponsible. Another key aspect of responsible disclosure is providing adequate time for the organization to develop and release a patch or mitigation for the vulnerability. The responsible party needs time to thoroughly investigate the issue, develop a fix, and test it to ensure it does not introduce new problems. Security researchers and ethical hackers typically agree on a reasonable timeframe for the organization to address the vulnerability before disclosing it publicly. This timeframe may vary depending on the severity of the vulnerability and the organization's ability to respond promptly. Responsible disclosure often involves cooperation between the security researcher or ethical hacker and the organization's security team. This collaboration can include sharing technical details of the vulnerability, providing proof-of-concept code, and assisting with the testing of patches or mitigations. Effective communication and collaboration help ensure that the vulnerability is understood and addressed correctly. Additionally, responsible disclosure emphasizes the importance of not exploiting or abusing the vulnerability for personal gain, malicious purposes, or any other harmful activities. Ethical hackers and security researchers adhere to a code of conduct that prioritizes the responsible handling of vulnerabilities. They refrain from taking advantage of the vulnerability to compromise systems, steal data, or engage in any malicious activities. Instead, they act in the best interest of improving cybersecurity and protecting users and organizations. Responsible disclosure also promotes transparency by allowing the organization to publicly acknowledge the vulnerability and the steps taken to address it. Once the organization has released a patch or mitigation for the vulnerability, it can provide users with information about the issue and the recommended actions to protect their systems. This transparency helps users understand the importance of applying updates and staying informed about security matters. In some cases, organizations may offer bug bounties or rewards to security researchers or ethical hackers who responsibly disclose vulnerabilities. These programs provide an incentive for individuals to report vulnerabilities, and they can result in valuable discoveries that enhance security. Bug bounty programs often have established guidelines and rules for reporting vulnerabilities and receiving rewards. Responsible disclosure is not limited to software vulnerabilities; it also applies to hardware, firmware, and systems. Whether it's a software bug, a hardware flaw, or a misconfiguration, responsible disclosure principles guide the reporting and remediation process. While responsible disclosure is a best practice in the cybersecurity community, not all organizations respond promptly or appropriately to vulnerability reports. Some organizations may not have established security processes, while others may downplay the severity of reported vulnerabilities. In such cases, security researchers and ethical hackers may face challenges in getting their concerns addressed. When faced with unresponsive organizations, some researchers choose to follow a process known as "full disclosure." Full disclosure involves publicly disclosing the vulnerability, along with technical details and proof-of-concept code, without waiting for the organization to respond. Full disclosure is considered a last resort and is typically only used when all attempts at responsible disclosure have failed, and there is a significant risk to users. It is important to note that full disclosure can have legal and ethical implications, and individuals should carefully consider the potential consequences before taking this step. In recent years, responsible disclosure has gained broader recognition, and many organizations have established formal channels for receiving vulnerability reports. These organizations recognize the value of collaboration with security researchers and ethical hackers in identifying and addressing security weaknesses. Some governments and industry groups have also issued guidelines and recommendations for responsible disclosure practices. Responsible disclosure is a critical element of the broader cybersecurity ecosystem, as it helps organizations protect their systems, data, and users from potential threats. It relies on the principles of transparency, collaboration, and responsible behavior to ensure that vulnerabilities are addressed promptly and effectively. Ultimately, responsible disclosure benefits everyone involved, as it contributes to a safer and more secure digital environment. Staying updated in cybersecurity is a constant and essential practice in a rapidly evolving digital landscape. Cyber threats and attack techniques are continually changing, making it imperative for cybersecurity professionals to remain knowledgeable about the latest developments. The importance of staying updated cannot be overstated, as outdated knowledge can lead to vulnerabilities and inadequate protection. One of the primary reasons for staying updated is to understand emerging cyber threats. New types of attacks and malware are constantly being developed by malicious actors seeking to exploit vulnerabilities. By staying informed about the latest threats, cybersecurity professionals can proactively prepare defenses and take measures to prevent attacks. Additionally, staying updated allows professionals to adapt their security strategies to the evolving threat landscape. Cybersecurity is a dynamic field, and what worked to protect systems and data yesterday may not be effective today. For example, new social engineering tactics or malware strains may require different defense strategies. Regularly reviewing threat intelligence feeds, cybersecurity news, and reports from security organizations is vital for staying informed about emerging threats. Staying updated is also essential for understanding the latest security vulnerabilities. Software and hardware vendors regularly release updates and patches to address security flaws. Cybersecurity professionals need to be aware of these vulnerabilities to ensure they apply patches promptly and mitigate potential risks. Failure to update software and systems in a timely manner can leave them exposed to exploitation by cybercriminals. Cybersecurity professionals should subscribe to vendor security advisories and monitor the Common Vulnerabilities and Exposures (CVE) database for information on newly discovered vulnerabilities. Moreover, staying updated is crucial for understanding evolving compliance requirements and regulations. Many industries are subject to specific cybersecurity regulations, such as the Health Insurance Portability and Accountability Act (HIPAA) or the General Data Protection Regulation (GDPR). These regulations can change over time, and organizations must stay updated to ensure they remain in compliance. Non-compliance can result in legal consequences and financial penalties. Furthermore, staying updated is essential for acquiring new skills and knowledge. Cybersecurity is a multidisciplinary field that encompasses a wide range of topics, from network security to cryptography and ethical hacking. As new technologies and techniques emerge, professionals may need to acquire new skills or certifications to stay relevant. Attending cybersecurity training courses, webinars, and conferences can help professionals acquire the latest knowledge and skills. Additionally, engaging in cybersecurity communities and forums allows individuals to share insights and learn from their peers. Staying updated is not limited to technical knowledge alone; it also includes understanding the human aspect of cybersecurity. Social engineering attacks, such as phishing and pretexting, continue to be effective tactics used by cybercriminals. Staying updated on the latest social engineering techniques helps individuals recognize and respond to these threats effectively. Another critical aspect of staying updated is understanding the evolving technology landscape. New technologies, such as cloud computing, the Internet of Things (IoT), and artificial intelligence (AI), introduce new security challenges. Cybersecurity professionals must be familiar with these technologies and their associated security implications. Adapting security strategies to protect cloud-based assets or IoT devices requires a deep understanding of their unique risks. Additionally, staying updated on industry best practices is essential for maintaining a strong security posture. Security frameworks and guidelines, such as the National Institute of Standards and Technology (NIST) Cybersecurity Framework or the Center for Internet Security (CIS) Controls, are regularly updated to address evolving threats. Implementing these best practices can help organizations establish a robust security foundation. Furthermore, staying updated is essential for incident response and threat hunting. In the event of a security incident, cybersecurity professionals need to rely on the latest knowledge and techniques to identify, contain, and mitigate the threat. Threat hunters actively search for signs of malicious activity within an organization's network, requiring a deep understanding of the latest attack techniques. Finally, staying updated fosters a culture of continuous improvement within cybersecurity teams. Cybersecurity professionals who prioritize learning and staying updated are more likely to be proactive in identifying and mitigating security risks. This proactive approach can lead to a more resilient security posture and reduced security incidents. In summary, staying updated in cybersecurity is an ongoing and critical practice for professionals and organizations alike. It involves staying informed about emerging threats, vulnerabilities, compliance requirements, and industry best practices. Staying updated also encompasses acquiring new skills, understanding evolving technologies, and fostering a culture of continuous improvement. By staying updated, cybersecurity professionals can better protect their organizations and respond effectively to the ever-changing cybersecurity landscape.

BOOK 2
MASTERING KALI LINUX NETHUNTER FOR WIRELESS SECURITY

ROB BOTWRIGHT

Chapter 1: Introduction to Kali Linux NetHunter

Kali Linux NetHunter is a specialized and powerful penetration testing platform designed for mobile devices. It is an extension of the popular Kali Linux distribution, which is widely used by cybersecurity professionals and ethical hackers for various security assessments and penetration testing activities. NetHunter is specifically tailored for mobile security testing and enables users to carry out security assessments on the go. This mobile penetration testing platform is compatible with a select range of Android devices, turning them into powerful hacking tools. Kali Linux NetHunter provides a comprehensive suite of security tools, allowing users to perform various tasks, such as wireless network analysis, vulnerability scanning, and ethical hacking. The primary focus of NetHunter is on wireless network security, making it an excellent choice for professionals who need to assess the security of Wi-Fi networks. One of the standout features of Kali Linux NetHunter is its integration with the Metasploit Framework, a well-known and versatile penetration testing tool. Metasploit offers a wide range of exploits, payloads, and modules for security testing and can be accessed directly through NetHunter. This integration enhances the capabilities of NetHunter, enabling users to launch sophisticated attacks and exploit vulnerabilities effectively. NetHunter also includes a powerful wireless attack toolkit that supports various wireless penetration testing activities. Users can leverage tools like Aircrack-ng, Reaver, and PixieWPS to assess the security of Wi-Fi networks, crack WEP and WPA/WPA2 keys, and test for vulnerabilities. The flexibility and portability of Kali Linux NetHunter make it an invaluable tool for security professionals, allowing them to conduct security assessments from virtually anywhere. NetHunter provides a user-friendly interface that simplifies the execution of complex security tasks, even for those who may not be experts in cybersecurity. It offers a streamlined and intuitive user experience, making it accessible to a wide range of users, from beginners to seasoned professionals. One of the key advantages of NetHunter is its ability to perform full-fledged security assessments on Android devices without the need for a separate laptop or computer. This makes it a practical solution for professionals who need to conduct on-site security assessments or remote testing. The NetHunter interface includes a menu of pre-installed security tools and scripts, organized by categories, making it easy to locate and execute the desired tool or command. Furthermore, NetHunter allows users to install additional packages and tools directly from the Kali Linux repository, expanding its functionality and versatility. In addition to its extensive wireless security capabilities, Kali Linux NetHunter offers a range of other penetration testing tools and utilities. These tools cover various aspects of security assessment, including web application testing, vulnerability scanning, and network analysis. Users can take advantage of tools like Burp Suite, Nikto, Nmap, and Wireshark to perform a wide array of security assessments. NetHunter also supports the use of external wireless adapters, such as Alfa Network's AWUS036ACH, to extend its wireless penetration testing capabilities. This flexibility allows users to choose the most suitable hardware for their specific testing needs. While Kali Linux NetHunter is a powerful platform for security assessments, it is important to note that its usage should always adhere to ethical and legal guidelines. Unauthorized penetration testing or hacking activities can lead to legal consequences and harm to individuals or organizations. Ethical hackers and security professionals should always obtain proper authorization and consent before conducting security assessments using NetHunter or any other tools. Furthermore, it is crucial to use NetHunter and its capabilities responsibly, with the utmost respect for privacy and the law. As technology continues to advance, the importance of mobile security testing becomes increasingly evident. With the proliferation of smartphones and mobile devices, the potential attack surface for cyber threats has expanded. Kali Linux NetHunter addresses this challenge by providing a comprehensive and accessible platform for assessing the security of mobile and wireless technologies. It empowers security professionals to identify vulnerabilities, test for weaknesses, and improve the overall security posture of mobile devices and wireless networks. In summary, Kali Linux NetHunter is a specialized penetration testing platform designed for mobile devices, offering a wide range of security tools and capabilities. It is an extension of the Kali Linux distribution and is specifically tailored for mobile security assessments. NetHunter's integration with the Metasploit Framework and its support for various wireless attack tools make it a powerful tool for cybersecurity professionals. Its user-friendly interface and portability make it accessible to both beginners and experts in the field. However, ethical and responsible usage is essential when conducting security assessments with NetHunter, and proper authorization and consent should always be obtained. Using Kali Linux NetHunter for wireless security assessments offers numerous benefits to cybersecurity professionals and ethical hackers. One of the primary advantages is its portability, as NetHunter transforms Android devices into powerful hacking tools, eliminating the need for a separate laptop or computer. This portability enables security assessments to be conducted on-site or remotely, enhancing the flexibility and convenience of security testing. NetHunter's integration with the Metasploit Framework provides users with access to a wide range of exploits, payloads, and modules for conducting sophisticated attacks and exploiting vulnerabilities effectively. This integration significantly enhances the capabilities of NetHunter and simplifies the execution of complex penetration testing tasks. Wireless network security is a focal point of Kali Linux NetHunter, making it an excellent choice for professionals needing to assess the security of Wi-Fi networks. The platform offers a comprehensive suite of wireless attack tools, such as Aircrack-ng, Reaver, and PixieWPS, for tasks like cracking WEP and WPA/WPA2 keys and testing for vulnerabilities. This robust toolkit enables thorough and effective wireless security assessments. Kali Linux NetHunter provides a user-friendly interface that streamlines the execution of security tasks, making it accessible to users with varying levels of expertise, from beginners to experienced professionals. The menu of pre-installed security tools and scripts is categorized for easy access and execution, simplifying the process of selecting the desired tool or command. Furthermore, users can expand NetHunter's functionality by installing additional packages and tools directly from the Kali Linux repository, offering versatility and customization. For professionals conducting on-site security assessments, Kali Linux NetHunter eliminates the need to carry a separate laptop or computer, resulting in a more streamlined and efficient testing process. The platform's interface and capabilities are designed to meet the needs of security professionals who require mobility and flexibility in their work. By providing a self-contained environment on Android devices, NetHunter enables security assessments to be performed wherever they are needed, whether in an office, data center, or remote location. NetHunter's support for external wireless adapters, such as Alfa Network's AWUS036ACH, extends its wireless penetration testing capabilities, allowing users to select the most suitable hardware for their specific testing requirements. This flexibility empowers security professionals to adapt to diverse wireless network environments and perform comprehensive assessments. In addition to wireless network security, Kali Linux NetHunter offers a range of other penetration testing tools and utilities, covering various aspects of security assessment, including web application testing, vulnerability scanning, and network analysis. Tools like Burp Suite, Nikto, Nmap, and Wireshark enable users to conduct a wide array of security assessments and identify vulnerabilities across different attack vectors. Despite its powerful capabilities, it is crucial to emphasize the ethical and responsible use of Kali Linux NetHunter. Unauthorized penetration testing or hacking activities can have legal consequences and cause harm to individuals and organizations. Security professionals and ethical hackers should always obtain proper authorization and consent before conducting security assessments using NetHunter or any other tools. Responsible and ethical behavior is essential in ensuring that security assessments contribute to improving security without causing harm or violating privacy. As technology continues to advance and the use of mobile and wireless devices becomes more prevalent, the importance of mobile security testing is evident. Kali Linux NetHunter addresses this need by providing a comprehensive and accessible platform for assessing the security of mobile devices and wireless networks. It equips security professionals with the tools and capabilities required to identify vulnerabilities, test for weaknesses, and enhance the overall security posture of these technologies. The integration with the Metasploit Framework and the extensive wireless attack toolkit make NetHunter a valuable asset for cybersecurity professionals, simplifying the process of conducting effective security assessments. In summary, the benefits of using Kali Linux NetHunter for wireless security assessments are substantial, ranging from portability and accessibility to a robust set of tools for conducting thorough and effective assessments. However, ethical and responsible usage is paramount to ensure that security assessments are conducted in a manner that respects legal and privacy considerations, obtaining proper authorization and consent when necessary.

Chapter 2: Setting Up Your NetHunter Environment

Installing Kali Linux NetHunter on mobile devices is a multi-step process that empowers users to transform their Android devices into powerful penetration testing tools. Before beginning the installation process, it is essential to ensure that the Android device meets the necessary prerequisites. The device should be rooted, which grants users administrative access to the device's operating system. Rooting an Android device may void warranties and should be done with caution. Once the device is rooted, users can proceed with installing a custom recovery tool, such as TWRP (Team Win Recovery Project), which is essential for the NetHunter installation process. After installing the custom recovery, users need to download the NetHunter ZIP file compatible with their specific device model and Android version. Kali Linux NetHunter offers official images for a select range of devices, and users should ensure that they download the correct image for their device. With the NetHunter ZIP file downloaded, users can transfer it to their Android device's storage, making it accessible during the installation process. The next step involves rebooting the device into recovery mode, which is typically done by powering off the device and then holding specific hardware buttons to access the custom recovery interface. Once in recovery mode, users can navigate to the "Install" or "Install ZIP" option and select the NetHunter ZIP file they transferred earlier. Confirming the installation prompts the custom recovery tool to flash NetHunter onto the device. The installation process may take some time, and users should wait patiently until it completes. After successfully installing NetHunter, users can reboot their Android device, and it will now run Kali Linux NetHunter alongside the existing Android operating system. Users can switch between the Android environment and NetHunter as needed, making it a versatile tool for security assessments. NetHunter provides a user-friendly interface that simplifies the execution of security tasks and offers a menu of pre-installed security tools and scripts organized by categories. The platform is designed to accommodate users with varying levels of expertise, from beginners to seasoned professionals. NetHunter's versatility extends to its support for external wireless adapters, allowing users to select the most suitable hardware for their specific testing requirements. External adapters, such as Alfa Network's AWUS036ACH, expand NetHunter's wireless penetration testing capabilities and empower users to adapt to diverse wireless network environments. Kali Linux NetHunter offers a wide range of security tools and utilities for various aspects of security assessment. It includes tools for wireless network analysis, vulnerability scanning, ethical hacking, and more. The integration with the Metasploit Framework enhances NetHunter's capabilities, providing users with access to a comprehensive suite of exploits, payloads, and modules for conducting advanced security assessments. NetHunter's wireless attack toolkit is another standout feature, enabling users to perform tasks like cracking WEP and WPA/WPA2 keys, testing for vulnerabilities, and conducting security assessments on Wi-Fi networks. The platform also supports the installation of additional packages and tools directly from the Kali Linux repository, offering customization and versatility. Despite its capabilities, it is crucial to highlight the importance of responsible and ethical usage when conducting security assessments with Kali Linux NetHunter. Unauthorized penetration testing or hacking activities can have serious legal consequences and cause harm to individuals or organizations. Security professionals and ethical hackers should always obtain proper authorization and consent before using NetHunter or any other tools for security assessments. Responsible and ethical behavior is paramount to ensure that security assessments are conducted in a manner that respects legal and privacy considerations. In summary, the installation of Kali Linux NetHunter on mobile devices empowers users to leverage their Android devices as powerful penetration testing tools. The process involves rooting the device, installing a custom recovery tool, and flashing the NetHunter ZIP file. Once installed, NetHunter provides a user-friendly interface, extensive security tools, and the flexibility to adapt to various wireless network environments. However, ethical and responsible usage is imperative to ensure that security assessments are conducted in compliance with legal and privacy standards.

Customizing your Kali Linux NetHunter environment allows you to tailor the platform to your specific needs and preferences. While NetHunter comes with a variety of pre-installed tools and scripts, customization enables you to add, remove, or configure elements to optimize your workflow. One of the first steps in customizing your NetHunter environment is installing additional packages and tools from the Kali Linux repository. These packages can expand the capabilities of NetHunter, providing you with more options for conducting security assessments. You can use the package manager, apt-get, to search for, install, and manage additional software packages. This allows you to add tools related to web application testing, network analysis, vulnerability scanning, and other security tasks. Customization also extends to modifying the appearance and layout of your NetHunter interface. You can personalize the graphical user interface (GUI) by changing themes, wallpapers, and icon sets to create an environment that suits your preferences. This level of customization enhances the overall user experience, making NetHunter more enjoyable and efficient to use. Furthermore, you can customize the NetHunter menu by organizing and categorizing tools and scripts according to your workflow. Rearranging menu items, adding shortcuts to frequently used tools, and creating custom categories help streamline navigation and access to essential resources. Another aspect of customization involves configuring and fine-tuning your wireless network setup. NetHunter provides support for external wireless adapters, allowing you to select the most suitable hardware for your wireless penetration testing needs. Configuring and optimizing the settings of these wireless adapters ensure that you can efficiently conduct security assessments on various wireless network environments. Moreover, you can customize your NetHunter environment by creating and storing scripts, templates, and configurations that align with your security testing methodologies. These scripts can automate repetitive tasks, save time, and ensure consistency in your assessments. For example, you can create scripts for specific reconnaissance activities, data analysis, or reporting, enhancing your efficiency during assessments. Customization also extends to your terminal emulator, allowing you to configure your preferred terminal application's appearance and behavior. You can set color schemes, fonts, keyboard shortcuts, and other settings to create a comfortable and efficient terminal environment. Furthermore, you can customize your shell environment by defining aliases, variables, and functions to simplify common tasks and commands. This level of customization enhances your productivity while working within the terminal. Managing and customizing your NetHunter environment can also involve creating and using custom profiles. Profiles allow you to configure and save specific settings for different types of assessments or scenarios. For example, you can create a profile for wireless penetration testing, another for web application assessments, and additional profiles for various clients or projects. Switching between profiles enables you to quickly load the appropriate settings, tools, and configurations for each scenario, saving time and ensuring consistency. Customizing your NetHunter environment includes optimizing your workspace by adjusting screen layouts, window positions, and panel configurations. This ensures that you have a clean and organized desktop that supports your workflow during security assessments. Customization also extends to the security configurations of your NetHunter environment. You can configure firewall rules, intrusion detection systems, and encryption settings to enhance the security of your testing environment. Customization of security configurations should align with ethical hacking practices and ensure the protection of your NetHunter system. Moreover, you can customize your NetHunter environment by creating and managing user accounts with appropriate permissions and access levels. This allows you to collaborate with other team members or grant limited access to specific resources while maintaining control over your environment. It's essential to regularly back up your customized NetHunter environment to prevent data loss or configuration errors. Creating backups of your system, configurations, scripts, and profiles ensures that you can restore your environment to a known and functional state in case of issues or failures. Customization also includes the ability to create documentation and notes within your NetHunter environment. You can use text editors, note-taking applications, or documentation tools to record findings, observations, and instructions during assessments. Having organized documentation readily available within your environment can improve communication, knowledge sharing, and the overall efficiency of your work. Customization is an ongoing process that adapts to your evolving needs, preferences, and security assessment methodologies. As you gain experience and encounter new challenges, you can continue to refine and optimize your NetHunter environment. Ultimately, customization enhances your productivity, efficiency, and effectiveness as a cybersecurity professional or ethical hacker. It enables you to create a tailored workspace that supports your unique requirements and maximizes your capabilities during security assessments. In summary, customizing your Kali Linux NetHunter environment is a valuable practice that empowers you to tailor the platform to your specific needs and preferences. Customization spans various aspects, including adding tools, configuring wireless adapters, personalizing the GUI, optimizing the terminal emulator, and creating scripts and profiles. It allows you to create a customized workspace that enhances your productivity, efficiency, and security during security assessments and penetration testing activities. Customization is an ongoing process that adapts to your evolving requirements and methodologies, ensuring that your NetHunter environment remains a powerful and versatile tool in your cybersecurity toolkit.

Chapter 3: Advanced Wi-Fi Scanning and Reconnaissance

In-depth Wi-Fi scanning techniques are a fundamental component of wireless security assessments and penetration testing. These techniques provide cybersecurity professionals and ethical hackers with the means to gather comprehensive information about wireless networks, their configurations, and potential vulnerabilities. One of the primary objectives of in-depth Wi-Fi scanning is to identify and map nearby wireless networks. This process involves detecting the presence of access points (APs), including both visible and hidden ones. Visible APs broadcast their presence through beacon frames, which contain essential information about the network, such as the SSID (Service Set Identifier) and supported security protocols. Hidden APs do not broadcast their SSID, making them less visible but still detectable through other means. The discovery of hidden APs is essential as they can potentially pose security risks if their configurations are weak or outdated. In addition to identifying APs, in-depth Wi-Fi scanning aims to gather detailed information about each network. This information includes the SSID, BSSID (Basic Service Set Identifier, which is the MAC address of the AP), channel, encryption type, signal strength, and supported authentication methods. Understanding these details is crucial for assessing the security posture of each network. Signal strength measurements help identify the physical location of APs and their approximate coverage areas. Knowing the signal strength can aid in locating rogue access points or unauthorized devices within a network.

Furthermore, in-depth Wi-Fi scanning includes the identification of the encryption and authentication methods used by each network. This information is vital for assessing the security level of a network and determining its susceptibility to various types of attacks. For example, networks using weak encryption methods like WEP (Wired Equivalent Privacy) are more vulnerable to attacks than those using stronger encryption like WPA2 (Wi-Fi Protected Access 2). Understanding the encryption method allows security professionals to prioritize their assessment efforts and tailor their attack strategies accordingly. In-depth Wi-Fi scanning also involves the detection of ESS (Extended Service Set) networks, which are composed of multiple APs that share the same SSID. Detecting ESS networks is essential for understanding the network infrastructure and potential attack surfaces. For instance, ESS networks may have roaming capabilities, which allow devices to seamlessly transition between APs as they move within the network. Roaming introduces security considerations, as attackers can exploit vulnerabilities during the handover process between APs. Another critical aspect of Wi-Fi scanning is the identification of client devices connected to each network. This includes both associated and unassociated devices. Associated devices are currently connected to the network, while unassociated devices may have previously connected or attempted to connect. Identifying client devices is crucial for understanding the composition of a network and assessing potential security risks. Furthermore, in-depth Wi-Fi scanning techniques include the collection of information about the network's operating mode and capabilities. This information encompasses details such as the supported data rates, modulation schemes, and supported standards (e.g., 802.11ac, 802.11n). Understanding a network's capabilities allows security professionals to tailor their assessments and target specific vulnerabilities or weaknesses. Channel utilization is another aspect of in-depth Wi-Fi scanning that provides valuable insights into network performance and potential interference. Analyzing channel utilization helps identify congested or crowded channels, which can impact network performance and security. Additionally, in-depth Wi-Fi scanning can reveal information about network security measures, such as the presence of intrusion detection systems (IDS) or intrusion prevention systems (IPS). Detecting these security measures is essential for ethical hackers to adapt their testing approaches and avoid triggering alarms or alerts. To perform in-depth Wi-Fi scanning effectively, security professionals and ethical hackers leverage specialized tools and software. These tools can perform active and passive scanning, probe for hidden networks, and provide detailed reports on network characteristics. One widely used tool for in-depth Wi-Fi scanning is Airodump-ng, which is part of the Aircrack-ng suite. Airodump-ng allows users to capture and analyze Wi-Fi traffic, providing detailed information about nearby networks and client devices. Other tools like Kismet, Wireshark, and NetStumbler also offer advanced scanning and analysis capabilities. Furthermore, in-depth Wi-Fi scanning can be complemented by hardware solutions, such as wireless network adapters with advanced monitoring and packet capture capabilities. These adapters allow security professionals to capture and analyze network traffic, helping to identify vulnerabilities and security weaknesses. In summary, in-depth Wi-Fi scanning techniques are a crucial component of wireless security assessments and penetration testing. These techniques involve the identification and detailed analysis of nearby wireless networks, their configurations, and potential vulnerabilities. In-depth scanning provides valuable insights into network composition, security measures, and potential attack surfaces. Using specialized tools and software, security professionals and ethical hackers can gather comprehensive information to assess and improve the security of wireless networks. Reconnaissance plays a pivotal role in the early stages of targeted cyberattacks, providing attackers with essential information to plan and execute their operations. Effective reconnaissance enables threat actors to gather intelligence about potential targets, including individuals, organizations, or systems. This gathered information serves as the foundation for crafting precise and tailored attack strategies. Targeted attacks, also known as advanced persistent threats (APTs), are sophisticated and stealthy in nature. They are designed to compromise specific targets with the aim of stealing sensitive data, intellectual property, or gaining unauthorized access to critical systems. Reconnaissance is the initial phase of a targeted attack, and its success greatly influences the success of the entire operation. One common objective of reconnaissance is to identify potential vulnerabilities and weaknesses within the target's infrastructure. This involves scanning for open ports, known vulnerabilities, misconfigured services, and outdated software. By identifying these weaknesses, attackers can determine potential entry points into the target's network or systems. Another key aspect of reconnaissance is the identification of key personnel within the target organization. This includes executives, IT administrators, and employees with access to sensitive data or critical systems. Knowing who holds key positions enables attackers to craft social engineering attacks or spear-phishing campaigns tailored to specific individuals. Additionally, reconnaissance aims to uncover the technology stack used by the target organization. This information helps attackers tailor their attacks to exploit known vulnerabilities in the software or hardware in use. Understanding the target's technology stack allows attackers to select the most effective attack vectors and tools. Social engineering attacks, which often rely on psychological manipulation and deception, are another component of reconnaissance. Attackers gather information about target employees, their roles, and their relationships within the organization. This information is then used to craft convincing phishing emails, pretexting scenarios, or impersonation tactics. The success of social engineering attacks often hinges on the accuracy and relevance of the gathered reconnaissance data. Open-source intelligence (OSINT) plays a significant role in reconnaissance for targeted attacks. Attackers leverage publicly available information from various sources, including social media, news articles, company websites, and online forums. This information can reveal details about the target's organizational structure, partnerships, recent events, and employee activities. Attackers may also monitor employee social media accounts to gather personal information that can be exploited in social engineering attacks. Reconnaissance activities also include probing the target's external perimeter to identify potential weaknesses. This involves scanning the target's public-facing servers, websites, and applications for vulnerabilities and misconfigurations. Attackers may employ automated scanning tools to discover open ports, exposed services, and known vulnerabilities. Once identified, these vulnerabilities can serve as entry points for the attacker to infiltrate the target's network. In addition to external reconnaissance, attackers may conduct internal reconnaissance to gather information once they have gained a foothold within the target's network. This phase involves mapping the internal network architecture, identifying critical systems, and locating valuable data repositories. Attackers may move laterally within the network to escalate privileges and identify high-value targets. Reconnaissance activities often go hand in hand with maintaining stealth and avoiding detection. Attackers take measures to cover their tracks, such as using anonymization techniques, employing encryption, and employing command-and-control (C2) infrastructure designed to evade detection. Moreover, reconnaissance is an ongoing process throughout the duration of a targeted attack. Attackers continuously gather and update information to adapt their tactics, techniques, and procedures (TTPs) based on changing circumstances. Defending against reconnaissance for targeted attacks is a complex and multifaceted challenge. Organizations must implement a robust cybersecurity strategy that includes proactive measures to detect and mitigate reconnaissance activities. This includes monitoring network traffic for suspicious patterns, identifying unauthorized access attempts, and implementing intrusion detection and prevention systems. User awareness training is crucial in preventing successful social engineering attacks. Employees should be educated about the risks of sharing sensitive information and trained to recognize phishing attempts and other manipulation tactics. Effective cybersecurity measures also involve keeping software and systems up to date, patching known vulnerabilities, and employing network segmentation to limit lateral movement within the network. Intrusion detection systems, threat intelligence feeds, and threat hunting practices can aid in identifying and responding to reconnaissance activities. Furthermore, organizations should establish an incident response plan to swiftly respond to any detected reconnaissance or security incidents. In summary, reconnaissance is a critical phase in targeted cyberattacks, providing attackers with vital information to plan and execute their operations. Effective reconnaissance enables attackers to identify vulnerabilities, target key personnel, and gather intelligence about the target organization. Defending against reconnaissance for targeted attacks requires a multifaceted cybersecurity strategy that includes monitoring, user education, patch management, network segmentation, and incident response preparedness.

Chapter 4: Cracking WPA/WPA2 Passwords with NetHunter

Preparing for WPA/WPA2 cracking is a crucial step in wireless security assessments and penetration testing, as these encryption protocols are commonly used to protect Wi-Fi networks. Before attempting to crack WPA/WPA2 keys, ethical hackers and cybersecurity professionals must gather the necessary tools and information. One essential tool for WPA/WPA2 cracking is Aircrack-ng, a suite of wireless network security tools that includes aircrack-ng, airmon-ng, and aireplay-ng. Aircrack-ng is a powerful tool for capturing packets, conducting attacks, and ultimately cracking WPA/WPA2 keys. In addition to Aircrack-ng, users should ensure that they have compatible wireless network adapters that support monitor mode and packet injection. Monitor mode allows the adapter to capture all wireless traffic on a specific channel, while packet injection enables the injection of specially crafted packets into the network. This functionality is essential for conducting the various stages of WPA/WPA2 cracking attacks. Choosing the right wireless network adapter is critical, as not all adapters are suitable for these tasks. Aircrack-ng maintains a list of compatible adapters on its website, which users can reference to ensure they have the appropriate hardware. To prepare for WPA/WPA2 cracking, it is crucial to identify the target network and gather relevant information about it. This includes the network's SSID (Service Set Identifier), BSSID (Basic Service Set Identifier), and channel information. The SSID is the network's name, while the BSSID is the MAC address of the access point (AP).

Channel information is necessary for selecting the correct channel to capture packets. In some cases, users may also need to determine the ESSID (Extended Service Set Identifier), which is the name of the network when hidden (not broadcasting). Knowing the target network's channel and BSSID is essential for efficient packet capture. Furthermore, it is crucial to gather information about the target network's encryption method and security settings. Determining whether the network uses WPA or WPA2, as well as the version (e.g., WPA2-PSK or WPA2-EAP), is vital for selecting the appropriate attack method. For example, WPA2-PSK networks use a pre-shared key, while WPA2-EAP networks require authentication with a central server. Knowing the encryption method helps ethical hackers tailor their attack strategy. Another important aspect of preparing for WPA/WPA2 cracking is the creation of a wordlist or dictionary. Wordlists contain a collection of potential passwords or passphrases that will be tested during the cracking process. Creating a high-quality wordlist is essential, as the success of WPA/WPA2 cracking largely depends on the strength and relevance of the words or phrases in the list. Wordlists can be generated manually, collected from publicly available sources, or compiled using specialized tools. To increase the chances of success, ethical hackers often create wordlists that include common passwords, dictionary words, and variations of known passphrases. Additionally, attackers may customize wordlists based on information gathered during reconnaissance, such as the target's interests, hobbies, or known phrases. Once all the necessary tools, hardware, and information are gathered, ethical hackers can proceed with capturing the

WPA/WPA2 handshake. The handshake is a critical step in the cracking process, as it captures the exchange of authentication messages between a client device and the access point. To capture the handshake, users typically employ a deauthentication attack (aireplay-ng) to force a client device to reauthenticate with the access point. This action triggers the handshake, which is then captured and saved for offline cracking. With the handshake captured, ethical hackers can use Aircrack-ng to initiate the WPA/WPA2 cracking process. Aircrack-ng, along with the captured handshake and wordlist, attempts to guess the network's pre-shared key by systematically testing each passphrase in the wordlist. The cracking process may take varying amounts of time depending on the complexity of the passphrase and the processing power available. To improve the efficiency of the cracking process, users can utilize a GPU (Graphics Processing Unit) for parallel processing, significantly speeding up the attack. Throughout the entire process of preparing for WPA/WPA2 cracking, ethical hackers must adhere to ethical guidelines and legal considerations. Gaining proper authorization and consent for conducting security assessments is paramount to ensure that the activity is conducted legally and ethically. Unauthorized penetration testing or hacking activities can lead to legal consequences and harm to individuals or organizations. Therefore, ethical hackers should always obtain permission from the network owner or responsible party before attempting any form of WPA/WPA2 cracking. Furthermore, ethical hackers should conduct their activities with the utmost professionalism, ensuring that their efforts are focused on improving security and identifying vulnerabilities. In summary, preparing for WPA/WPA2 cracking is a critical aspect of wireless security assessments and penetration testing. It involves gathering the necessary tools, information, and hardware, as well as creating a high-quality wordlist. The process also includes capturing the WPA/WPA2 handshake, which is a crucial step in offline cracking. Ethical hackers must always adhere to ethical guidelines, obtain proper authorization, and conduct their activities in a legal and responsible manner. Preparing for WPA/WPA2 cracking requires careful planning and execution to ensure successful and ethical security assessments.

Executing WPA/WPA2 attacks with Kali Linux NetHunter is a specialized skill that allows ethical hackers and cybersecurity professionals to assess and test the security of wireless networks. NetHunter, a powerful penetration testing platform, provides a range of tools and utilities designed for conducting various wireless security assessments, including WPA/WPA2 attacks. Before proceeding with WPA/WPA2 attacks, users must ensure they have the necessary hardware and software components in place. This includes a compatible mobile device with NetHunter installed, a compatible wireless network adapter, and a well-prepared wordlist for passphrase cracking. NetHunter offers a user-friendly interface that simplifies the process of configuring and launching WPA/WPA2 attacks. One of the most commonly used tools for WPA/WPA2 attacks in NetHunter is Aircrack-ng, a versatile suite of wireless network security tools. Aircrack-ng includes utilities such as aircrack-ng (for passphrase cracking), airmon-ng (for interface management), and aireplay-ng (for packet injection and deauthentication attacks). To begin, users must first launch the NetHunter app on their mobile device and ensure that their wireless network adapter is recognized and operational. The wireless network adapter should support monitor mode and packet injection, as these functionalities are crucial for conducting WPA/WPA2 attacks. Once the wireless network adapter is ready, users can use the NetHunter interface to start monitoring nearby wireless networks and identify their SSIDs and BSSIDs. The SSID, or Service Set Identifier, is the name of the wireless network, while the BSSID, or Basic Service Set Identifier, is the MAC address of the access point (AP). This information is essential for targeting a specific network during the attack. After identifying the target network, users can proceed with capturing the WPA/WPA2 handshake. The handshake is a critical component in the passphrase cracking process, as it represents the exchange of authentication messages between a client device and the AP. To capture the handshake, ethical hackers often use a deauthentication attack, sending deauthentication packets to a connected client device to force it to reauthenticate with the AP. Once the client device reauthenticates, the handshake is captured and saved for offline cracking. With the captured handshake in hand, users can employ Aircrack-ng to launch a dictionary-based attack on the target network. Aircrack-ng uses a wordlist, containing potential passphrases, to systematically test each passphrase against the captured handshake. The cracking process continues until a matching passphrase is found or until the entire wordlist is exhausted. The success of the attack largely depends on the quality of the wordlist and the complexity of the passphrase. Ethical hackers often create or use customized wordlists that include common passwords, dictionary words, and variations of known passphrases. Additionally, they may craft wordlists tailored to the specific target network, incorporating information gathered during reconnaissance. To improve the efficiency of the passphrase cracking process, users can leverage the processing power of GPUs (Graphics Processing Units) for parallel processing. This significantly speeds up the attack by testing multiple passphrases simultaneously. NetHunter provides support for GPU acceleration, allowing users to take advantage of this capability. Ethical hackers must always operate within the boundaries of ethical guidelines and legal considerations when executing WPA/WPA2 attacks. Obtaining proper authorization and consent from the network owner or responsible party is crucial to ensure that the activity is conducted legally and ethically. Unauthorized penetration testing or hacking activities can have legal consequences and may cause harm to individuals or organizations. Therefore, ethical hackers should always exercise professionalism and prioritize improving security while identifying vulnerabilities. It is important to note that the knowledge and skills required for executing WPA/WPA2 attacks should only be used for legitimate security assessments and testing purposes. Misuse of these techniques for malicious activities is illegal and unethical. In summary, executing WPA/WPA2 attacks with Kali Linux NetHunter is a specialized skill that allows ethical hackers and cybersecurity professionals to assess wireless network security. NetHunter, equipped with tools like Aircrack-ng, provides a user-friendly interface for conducting WPA/WPA2 attacks. Users must ensure they have the necessary hardware and wordlists, capture the handshake, and employ ethical practices throughout the process. Executing WPA/WPA2 attacks requires careful planning, ethical considerations, and adherence to legal guidelines to ensure responsible security assessments.

Chapter 5: Wireless Exploitation with NetHunter Tools

Utilizing NetHunter tools for exploits is a critical aspect of conducting ethical hacking and penetration testing on wireless networks. Kali Linux NetHunter, a powerful mobile penetration testing platform, offers a wide range of tools and utilities that enable ethical hackers and cybersecurity professionals to identify and exploit vulnerabilities in target systems. Before delving into the specifics of utilizing NetHunter tools for exploits, it is essential to emphasize the importance of ethical hacking practices and obtaining proper authorization for security assessments. Unauthorized or malicious exploitation of vulnerabilities can lead to legal consequences and harm to individuals or organizations. Ethical hackers must operate within the boundaries of legal and ethical guidelines, obtaining consent from the network owner or responsible party before conducting security assessments. With proper authorization in place, ethical hackers can leverage NetHunter's capabilities to assess and improve the security of wireless networks. One of the fundamental steps in utilizing NetHunter tools for exploits is the initial reconnaissance phase. Reconnaissance involves gathering information about the target network, including details about the network's configuration, devices, and potential vulnerabilities. This information serves as the foundation for selecting the appropriate tools and exploitation techniques. NetHunter provides a suite of tools for conducting reconnaissance, including utilities like Nmap for network scanning, Wireshark for packet analysis, and Airodump-ng for wireless network discovery. These tools help ethical hackers identify open ports, active services, and potential entry points within the target network. Once the reconnaissance phase is complete, ethical hackers can move on to the exploitation phase. NetHunter offers a variety of tools for exploiting different types of vulnerabilities, ranging from network-level vulnerabilities to application-level weaknesses. One of the key tools for exploiting wireless network vulnerabilities is Metasploit, a widely-used penetration testing framework that is included in Kali Linux. Metasploit provides a vast array of modules and payloads designed to exploit known vulnerabilities in target systems. Ethical hackers can utilize Metasploit to perform a wide range of attacks, including remote code execution, privilege escalation, and post-exploitation activities. In the context of wireless network exploitation, Metasploit modules can be used to target vulnerable services, devices, or applications within the network. For example, if a known vulnerability exists in a wireless router's firmware, ethical hackers can search for and use Metasploit modules that specifically target that vulnerability. Additionally, NetHunter provides tools like WiFite and Fern-WiFi-Cracker that focus on exploiting weaknesses in WEP, WPA, and WPA2 encryption protocols. These tools automate the process of capturing handshakes, conducting deauthentication attacks, and attempting to crack Wi-Fi passwords. Ethical hackers can leverage these tools to assess the security of Wi-Fi networks and identify weaknesses that may be exploited by malicious actors. While exploring NetHunter tools for exploits, ethical hackers must also consider the importance of post-exploitation activities. Once a successful exploitation has occurred, ethical hackers gain access to the target system and should proceed with caution and professionalism. Post-exploitation activities involve maintaining access, escalating privileges, and conducting further assessments to identify additional vulnerabilities within the network. NetHunter tools, such as Meterpreter, enable ethical hackers to establish a reverse shell or persistent backdoor on the compromised system. This provides a means of maintaining access and conducting reconnaissance within the network. Furthermore, ethical hackers can utilize NetHunter tools like SniffAir for conducting wireless network reconnaissance after gaining access to the target network. This tool helps identify additional devices, services, and potential attack vectors within the network. Another important aspect of utilizing NetHunter tools for exploits is staying informed about the latest vulnerabilities and security updates. Ethical hackers should regularly update their knowledge and toolsets to ensure they are equipped to identify and exploit new vulnerabilities as they emerge. This involves staying up-to-date with security news, advisories, and research findings in the cybersecurity field. Additionally, ethical hackers can subscribe to security mailing lists, forums, and communities to collaborate with peers and share knowledge. To conclude, utilizing NetHunter tools for exploits is a vital component of ethical hacking and penetration testing in the context of wireless networks. Ethical hackers must operate within legal and ethical boundaries, obtain proper authorization, and follow responsible security assessment practices. NetHunter offers a comprehensive set of tools for reconnaissance, exploitation, and post-exploitation activities, allowing ethical hackers to assess and improve the security of wireless networks. Staying informed about the latest vulnerabilities and security updates is essential for ethical hackers to remain effective and adaptive in their role. Exploiting wireless vulnerabilities is a critical aspect of ethical hacking and cybersecurity assessments, focusing on identifying weaknesses in wireless networks and systems. Wireless networks are prevalent in today's digital landscape, offering convenience and connectivity but also introducing security challenges and potential vulnerabilities. Ethical hackers, often referred to as white-hat hackers or security professionals, play a crucial role in uncovering these vulnerabilities before malicious actors can exploit them. The exploitation of wireless vulnerabilities requires a systematic approach, including reconnaissance, vulnerability analysis, and responsible disclosure. Reconnaissance, the first phase of the process, involves gathering information about the target wireless network, such as its SSID (Service Set Identifier), BSSID (Basic Service Set Identifier), encryption protocols, and potential entry points. This information helps ethical hackers understand the network's configuration and potential weaknesses. Vulnerability analysis is the next step, where ethical hackers use various tools and techniques to identify vulnerabilities within the wireless network. Common vulnerabilities in wireless networks include weak encryption, default credentials, misconfigured access points, and outdated firmware. Ethical hackers leverage their knowledge and expertise to pinpoint these vulnerabilities and assess their potential impact on the network's security. The use of specialized tools, like Aircrack-ng and Wireshark, aids in capturing packets, analyzing network traffic, and identifying potential weaknesses. Once vulnerabilities are identified, ethical hackers proceed with responsible disclosure, a critical ethical consideration in the exploitation process. Responsible disclosure involves notifying the network owner or administrator about the discovered vulnerabilities and providing guidance on mitigating the risks. This ethical approach ensures that vulnerabilities are addressed promptly, enhancing overall network security and reducing the likelihood of malicious exploitation. To exploit wireless vulnerabilities effectively, ethical hackers employ various techniques and tools tailored to the specific weaknesses they have identified. One common vulnerability in wireless networks is the use of weak encryption protocols, such as

WEP (Wired Equivalent Privacy). WEP is known for its vulnerabilities, and ethical hackers can exploit these weaknesses by capturing data packets and using tools like Aircrack-ng to crack WEP keys. Cracking WEP keys grants unauthorized access to the network, highlighting the importance of using stronger encryption methods like WPA2 (Wi-Fi Protected Access 2). Default credentials on wireless devices, such as routers and access points, present another exploitable vulnerability. Ethical hackers may attempt to gain access to these devices using default usernames and passwords, which are often well-documented and publicly available. By accessing the device's configuration settings, ethical hackers can potentially manipulate network settings, intercept traffic, or compromise the network's security. Misconfigured access points are also prime targets for exploitation. Ethical hackers look for access points with weak security configurations, such as open networks with no encryption or weak authentication methods. Exploiting these misconfigurations allows attackers to gain unauthorized access to the network and potentially intercept sensitive data. Furthermore, ethical hackers pay close attention to devices with outdated firmware or software, as these may contain known vulnerabilities that can be exploited. They may use tools like Nessus or OpenVAS to scan the network for devices with outdated software and subsequently target them for exploitation. Once a vulnerability is successfully exploited, ethical hackers can gain unauthorized access to the network or compromise specific systems or devices. For example, if an attacker exploits a weak encryption vulnerability, they can intercept and decrypt network traffic, potentially exposing sensitive information. Additionally, compromising network devices can lead to unauthorized control over access points or routers, allowing attackers to manipulate network settings or launch more extensive attacks. Ethical hackers often document their findings and share them with the network owner or administrator, enabling timely remediation and strengthening the network's security. In summary, exploiting wireless vulnerabilities is a critical component of ethical hacking and cybersecurity assessments. Ethical hackers systematically identify weaknesses in wireless networks, including weak encryption, default credentials, misconfigured access points, and outdated firmware. Using specialized tools and techniques, they exploit these vulnerabilities to assess their impact and provide responsible disclosure to enhance network security. By uncovering and addressing vulnerabilities proactively, ethical hackers play a crucial role in safeguarding wireless networks from malicious exploitation.

Chapter 6: Advanced Wi-Fi Attacks and Mitigations

Advanced attack techniques with Kali Linux NetHunter represent the pinnacle of ethical hacking capabilities, enabling cybersecurity professionals to assess and exploit complex vulnerabilities in wireless networks and systems. These advanced techniques are reserved for experienced professionals who have mastered the fundamentals of ethical hacking and possess the knowledge and skills required for intricate network penetration. In the realm of wireless network security, attackers continuously evolve their tactics to overcome ever-improving defenses, making it essential for ethical hackers to stay ahead of the curve. Advanced attack techniques encompass a wide range of approaches and strategies, each designed to exploit specific weaknesses in wireless networks. One such advanced technique involves leveraging vulnerabilities in wireless protocols or devices to gain unauthorized access or control over network resources. This may include exploiting weaknesses in outdated authentication mechanisms, such as WEP, or identifying vulnerabilities in the implementation of newer protocols like WPA3. Advanced attackers can use custom scripts or tools to target these vulnerabilities, enabling them to bypass security measures and compromise network integrity. Another advanced attack technique involves the manipulation of wireless clients to connect to rogue access points controlled by attackers. By setting up malicious access points with enticing SSIDs, attackers can trick unsuspecting clients into connecting to them, potentially exposing sensitive information. Advanced attackers can automate this process using tools like Fluxion or create custom scripts to make rogue access points appear more legitimate. Additionally, advanced attackers often employ techniques to evade intrusion detection systems (IDS) and intrusion prevention systems (IPS) that may be in place within the target network. This includes crafting packets in a way that avoids detection by signature-based IDS/IPS or disguising malicious traffic as legitimate communication. Sophisticated attackers may utilize packet fragmentation, encryption, or tunneling techniques to obfuscate their activities and avoid triggering alerts. Furthermore, advanced attack techniques may involve the exploitation of zero-day vulnerabilities—previously unknown weaknesses in software or hardware. Ethical hackers with knowledge of zero-day vulnerabilities can use them to gain unauthorized access to networks and systems before patches or updates are available to protect against such attacks. However, it is essential to highlight that responsible disclosure of zero-day vulnerabilities is a critical ethical consideration. Ethical hackers must work with vendors and authorities to ensure that vulnerabilities are patched promptly and do not pose a significant threat to the wider community. One advanced technique that ethical hackers frequently employ is the use of privilege escalation exploits. These exploits target weaknesses in operating systems, applications, or services to gain elevated privileges, enabling attackers to execute commands or access resources beyond their initial level of access. Advanced attackers can identify and exploit privilege escalation vulnerabilities to gain full control over compromised systems or networks. Additionally, ethical hackers often engage in post-exploitation activities, leveraging advanced techniques to maintain persistence and continue their reconnaissance efforts within the target network. This may involve the deployment of rootkits, backdoors, or persistence mechanisms that ensure access even if the initial point of entry is discovered and closed. Advanced attackers prioritize covering their tracks and erasing evidence of their presence in the compromised environment. They may employ anti-forensic techniques to make it challenging for forensic investigators to trace their activities or recover deleted data. These techniques include overwriting data, modifying timestamps, and utilizing secure deletion tools. Furthermore, ethical hackers with advanced skill sets may engage in advanced social engineering tactics, such as spear phishing or pretexting, to manipulate individuals within the target organization. By crafting convincing social engineering campaigns, attackers can trick employees into disclosing sensitive information, providing access credentials, or executing malicious code. Advanced attackers combine technical prowess with psychological manipulation to achieve their objectives. It is crucial to emphasize that advanced attack techniques are reserved for ethical hacking and cybersecurity professionals who conduct authorized security assessments. Engaging in malicious or unauthorized activities, even with advanced skills, is illegal and unethical. Ethical hackers must adhere to ethical guidelines, obtain proper authorization, and prioritize improving security while identifying vulnerabilities. Moreover, ethical hackers should continuously update their knowledge and skills to adapt to evolving threats and defense mechanisms. In summary, advanced attack techniques with Kali Linux NetHunter represent the highest level of ethical hacking expertise. These techniques encompass a wide range of approaches, including exploiting wireless vulnerabilities, manipulating clients, evading intrusion detection systems, leveraging zero-day vulnerabilities, and conducting privilege escalation exploits. Ethical hackers with advanced skills play a crucial role in identifying and addressing security weaknesses in wireless networks and systems while adhering to ethical guidelines and responsible disclosure practices. Countermeasures against Wi-Fi attacks are vital for organizations and individuals looking to protect their wireless networks and maintain the confidentiality, integrity, and availability of their data. As wireless technology continues to advance, so do the techniques and tools used by attackers to exploit vulnerabilities in Wi-Fi networks. To effectively defend against these threats, it is essential to employ a multi-layered approach that encompasses both technical and procedural countermeasures. One fundamental countermeasure is the use of strong encryption protocols, such as WPA3 (Wi-Fi Protected Access 3), to secure Wi-Fi communications. WPA3 offers enhanced security features, including stronger encryption algorithms and protection against brute-force attacks. By using the latest encryption standards, organizations can significantly reduce the risk of data interception and unauthorized access to their Wi-Fi networks. Another crucial countermeasure is the regular patching and updating of Wi-Fi network devices, including routers, access points, and client devices. Vendors release firmware and software updates to address known vulnerabilities and improve the security of their products. Failing to apply these updates can leave Wi-Fi networks susceptible to exploitation, as attackers may target known weaknesses. Furthermore, organizations should employ strong and unique passwords for their Wi-Fi networks, changing them periodically and ensuring that default passwords are never used. Weak or commonly used passwords are easy targets for attackers using dictionary attacks or password-cracking tools. Implementing a robust password policy can significantly enhance network security. Network segmentation is an effective countermeasure that involves dividing a Wi-Fi network into distinct segments or VLANs (Virtual Local Area Networks). Each segment may have its own security policies and access controls. By segmenting the network, even if an attacker gains access to one segment, they will have limited visibility and access to other parts of the network. Additionally, organizations should implement strong access controls, including role-based access control (RBAC) and least privilege access principles. These measures restrict users' access to network resources based on their roles and permissions, reducing the attack surface and minimizing the potential impact of a breach. To defend against rogue access points, organizations can use wireless intrusion detection systems (WIDS) to monitor the network for unauthorized or malicious devices. WIDS solutions can identify and alert administrators to the presence of rogue access points, allowing for swift remediation. Network monitoring and analysis tools, such as Wireshark, can also aid in identifying unusual or suspicious network traffic patterns that may indicate an ongoing attack. Implementing strong physical security measures is equally important in defending against Wi-Fi attacks. Organizations should ensure that physical access to network equipment and wiring is restricted to authorized personnel only. Physical security controls, such as locked server rooms and access card systems, help prevent unauthorized individuals from tampering with network infrastructure. Regular security assessments and penetration testing can help organizations identify vulnerabilities and weaknesses in their Wi-Fi networks. By conducting ethical hacking tests, organizations can proactively address security issues before attackers have a chance to exploit them. Intrusion detection and prevention systems (IDS/IPS) play a crucial role in identifying and blocking malicious activity within Wi-Fi networks. These systems analyze network traffic, looking for patterns and anomalies that may indicate an attack or intrusion. Intrusion prevention systems can take automated actions to block or mitigate threats as they are detected. Implementing network segmentation, isolating sensitive systems from public Wi-Fi networks, and using strong network access controls can limit an attacker's ability to move laterally within the network if they gain access. Employee training and awareness programs are essential countermeasures against Wi-Fi attacks. Employees should be educated about the risks of connecting to unsecured Wi-Fi networks and the importance of following security policies and best practices. Phishing awareness training can help employees recognize social engineering attempts that may lead to Wi-Fi network compromises. Regularly reviewing and updating security policies and procedures to address evolving threats is crucial. Organizations should establish an incident response plan that outlines the steps to take in the event of a Wi-Fi security breach. This plan should include procedures for identifying the extent of the breach, containing the incident, mitigating damage, and notifying affected parties. It is also essential to maintain logs and records of network activity, as these can provide valuable information for investigating and responding to security incidents. Furthermore, organizations should consider the use of network access control (NAC) solutions that assess the security posture of devices attempting to connect to the Wi-Fi network. NAC systems can enforce security policies and ensure that only compliant and authorized devices gain access. Regular security audits and assessments by third-party experts can provide organizations with an objective evaluation of their Wi-Fi security posture. These assessments can uncover vulnerabilities and weaknesses that may have been overlooked. Lastly, organizations should establish a culture of security awareness and accountability, where all employees understand their role in maintaining Wi-Fi network security. This culture can help prevent security lapses and improve the overall security posture of the organization. In summary, countermeasures against Wi-Fi attacks are crucial for safeguarding wireless networks from evolving threats. A multi-layered approach that combines technical measures, procedural policies, and employee awareness is essential for comprehensive network security. By implementing strong encryption, keeping devices up to date, using robust access controls, and conducting regular security assessments, organizations can significantly reduce their exposure to Wi-Fi attacks and maintain the integrity of their networks.

Chapter 7: Network Sniffing and Packet Analysis

Capturing and analyzing network traffic is a fundamental practice in the field of cybersecurity, providing valuable insights into the behavior of networked systems and potential security threats. Network traffic encompasses the flow of data packets between devices connected to a network, including local area networks (LANs), wide area networks (WANs), and the internet. Analyzing this traffic helps cybersecurity professionals understand how data is transmitted, identify patterns, and detect abnormal or malicious activities. One of the primary purposes of capturing network traffic is to monitor network performance and troubleshoot connectivity issues. By examining the flow of data packets, network administrators can identify bottlenecks, latency, and packet loss that may be affecting network performance. This data-driven approach allows them to make informed decisions and optimize the network infrastructure for efficiency. Furthermore, capturing network traffic is essential for ensuring the security of networked systems. Cyberattacks often involve the transmission of malicious packets or unusual traffic patterns that can be detected through traffic analysis. Security professionals use network packet capture tools to monitor for signs of unauthorized access, data breaches, and other security incidents. Packet capture tools, such as Wireshark, Tcpdump, and Snort, record network traffic in real-time or save it for later analysis. These tools provide detailed information about each packet, including source and destination addresses, protocols used, packet size, and timestamp. Network analysts can use this data to investigate incidents, identify potential threats, and take appropriate remedial actions. Analyzing network traffic is an essential component of intrusion detection systems (IDS) and intrusion prevention systems (IPS). These security solutions monitor network traffic for suspicious or malicious activity and use predefined rules and signatures to identify potential threats. When an IDS or IPS detects anomalous behavior, it can trigger alerts or take automated actions to block or mitigate the threat. Packet capture plays a crucial role in providing the data necessary for IDS and IPS systems to analyze and detect network intrusions. Deep packet inspection (DPI) is a technique used to inspect the content of data packets at a granular level. DPI examines the payload of packets to identify specific applications, protocols, or even malware signatures. This level of analysis can help security professionals understand the nature of the traffic on their network and identify malicious activity or policy violations. While capturing and analyzing network traffic, it is essential to consider privacy and compliance regulations. In many regions and industries, there are strict data protection laws that govern the collection and storage of network data, particularly if it contains sensitive or personal information. Organizations must implement appropriate measures, such as encryption and access controls, to protect captured network data from unauthorized access or disclosure. Additionally, it is crucial to retain network traffic data only for the necessary duration to meet regulatory requirements. Retaining data for longer than necessary increases the risk of data breaches and potential legal liabilities. Intrusion detection and prevention are not the only security applications of traffic analysis. Network traffic analysis can also be used for forensic purposes. When a security incident occurs, analysts can review captured traffic data to reconstruct events, identify the source of an attack, and understand the extent of the damage. This forensic analysis is crucial for incident response and legal investigations. Network traffic analysis also plays a pivotal role in identifying and mitigating distributed denial of service (DDoS) attacks. By monitoring traffic patterns and identifying abnormal surges in traffic volume, DDoS attacks can be detected and mitigated in real-time to ensure network availability. Furthermore, traffic analysis can be used to detect and prevent data exfiltration attempts. Cybercriminals often attempt to exfiltrate sensitive data from a compromised network by disguising it within normal traffic patterns. Traffic analysis tools can identify anomalies in data flows and raise alerts when suspicious data transfers are detected. In summary, capturing and analyzing network traffic is a fundamental practice for monitoring network performance, ensuring cybersecurity, and investigating security incidents. Through the use of packet capture tools, security professionals can gain valuable insights into network behavior, detect anomalies and threats, and take proactive measures to protect networked systems. However, it is essential to balance the benefits of traffic analysis with privacy considerations and compliance requirements to maintain data security and legal compliance.

Deep Packet Inspection (DPI) is a powerful network analysis technique that allows for in-depth examination of the content of data packets traversing a network.

Wireshark, a widely-used open-source packet capture and analysis tool, provides the means to perform DPI and gain valuable insights into network traffic. DPI goes beyond traditional packet analysis by examining the payload of data packets, allowing for the inspection of application-layer data and the identification of specific protocols and even malware signatures. This granular level of inspection makes DPI a critical tool for network administrators, security professionals, and forensic analysts. Wireshark, formerly known as Ethereal, is a versatile tool that supports DPI across various network protocols, making it suitable for a wide range of applications. To perform DPI with Wireshark effectively, one must understand the tool's capabilities, features, and best practices. One of the key advantages of Wireshark is its ability to capture network traffic in real-time or analyze pre-recorded capture files. This flexibility allows security professionals to monitor live network activity and perform retrospective analysis of historical data. When analyzing network traffic with Wireshark, it's essential to start with a clear objective. Are you looking to troubleshoot network performance issues, detect security threats, or investigate a specific incident? Defining your goals helps you focus your analysis and efficiently filter the relevant packets from the vast amount of data captured. Filters in Wireshark are powerful tools that enable users to narrow down their analysis to specific packets or protocols of interest. Creating custom filters based on criteria such as source or destination IP addresses, port numbers, or protocol types can streamline the DPI process. Wireshark's display filters provide a visual representation of the filtered packets, making it easier to identify patterns or anomalies. To perform DPI effectively, it's crucial to stay updated with the latest Wireshark releases, as new versions often include enhancements and bug fixes that improve the tool's functionality. Wireshark also offers the capability to decrypt encrypted traffic if the appropriate keys or certificates are available. This feature is particularly useful for analyzing secure communications, but it requires access to the encryption keys used in the communication. Wireshark's extensive protocol support is a significant advantage when conducting DPI. The tool can dissect and analyze a wide range of network protocols, including HTTP, FTP, SMTP, DNS, and many more. This capability allows analysts to understand how different applications and services interact on the network. Identifying abnormal or unauthorized protocols within the traffic can be a crucial aspect of security monitoring. While DPI is a powerful technique, it is essential to use it responsibly and consider privacy concerns and legal implications. DPI can reveal sensitive information within network traffic, including usernames, passwords, and personally identifiable information (PII). As such, capturing and analyzing network traffic should always adhere to privacy regulations and organizational policies. In some cases, anonymizing or pseudonymizing data may be necessary to protect sensitive information during analysis. Moreover, DPI should be performed only on networks and traffic for which you have explicit authorization. Unauthorized packet inspection can violate privacy rights and legal regulations. DPI with Wireshark can be applied to various use cases, including network troubleshooting, security monitoring, and forensic analysis. Network administrators often use Wireshark to diagnose connectivity issues, identify network bottlenecks, and optimize network performance. Security professionals leverage Wireshark to detect and investigate security incidents, such as malware infections, data breaches, and suspicious network behavior. Wireshark's ability to analyze encrypted traffic is particularly valuable in identifying malicious activities that attempt to hide within secure channels. Forensic analysts rely on Wireshark to reconstruct events, gather evidence, and establish timelines during investigations. The tool helps them understand the sequence of actions that occurred within a networked environment. In summary, Deep Packet Inspection (DPI) with Wireshark is a valuable technique for examining network traffic at a granular level. Wireshark's extensive protocol support, filtering capabilities, and real-time and retrospective analysis options make it a versatile tool for network administrators, security professionals, and forensic analysts. However, it is essential to use DPI responsibly, following privacy regulations and organizational policies, and ensuring that authorization is obtained for any packet inspection activities.

Chapter 8: Leveraging NetHunter for Mobile Security Assessments

Assessing mobile devices and apps has become increasingly critical as smartphones and tablets have become ubiquitous in our daily lives. Mobile devices have evolved into powerful computing platforms that store sensitive information and provide access to a wide range of applications and services. This evolution has also made them attractive targets for cyberattacks and data breaches. To ensure the security and privacy of both personal and business data, it is essential to conduct thorough assessments of mobile devices and the apps they run. Mobile device assessments typically involve evaluating the security of the hardware, operating system, and the applications installed on the device. One of the primary considerations when assessing mobile devices is the device's physical security. This includes assessing the physical integrity of the device, ensuring that it has not been tampered with or compromised in any way. Physical security assessments also involve examining the device's locking mechanisms, such as biometric authentication (e.g., fingerprint or facial recognition) and PIN or password protection. In addition to physical security, the operating system of the mobile device plays a crucial role in its overall security posture. Assessments should include a review of the device's operating system and its security features. Security features may include secure boot processes, encryption capabilities, and the ability to install security patches and updates. Regularly updating the operating system is essential to address known vulnerabilities and protect against emerging threats. Mobile apps are another critical component of the assessment process. Apps can pose security risks if they have vulnerabilities or are granted excessive permissions. Assessing mobile apps involves examining their source code or binary files, analyzing their network communication, and evaluating their data storage practices. Mobile app assessments should identify potential security issues, such as insecure data storage, insecure communication, and weak authentication mechanisms. Permissions granted to apps should be reviewed to ensure they are appropriate and necessary for the app's functionality. Another important aspect of mobile device assessments is the evaluation of mobile device management (MDM) solutions. MDM solutions are used by organizations to manage and secure mobile devices used by their employees. Assessments of MDM solutions should focus on their ability to enforce security policies, remotely wipe or lock devices, and monitor device compliance. Mobile device assessments should also consider the use of mobile application management (MAM) solutions. MAM solutions enable organizations to manage and secure mobile apps deployed on employees' devices. Evaluating MAM solutions involves assessing their ability to control app distribution, enforce security policies, and protect app data. Mobile devices often have access to sensitive corporate data and resources, making them attractive targets for attackers. To protect against potential threats, organizations should implement secure network configurations and enforce strict access controls. Assessments should include a review of network security settings, such as Wi-Fi and cellular connectivity, as well as the use of virtual private networks (VPNs) and firewall rules. Security configurations should be tailored to the organization's specific requirements and risk profile. Mobile devices are frequently used to access corporate email, calendars, and other business-critical applications. Assessments should examine the security of email and communication applications, ensuring that they use secure protocols for data transmission and storage. Mobile device assessments should also consider the potential risks associated with the use of public Wi-Fi networks. Public Wi-Fi networks are often less secure than private networks and can expose devices to various security threats, such as eavesdropping and man-in-the-middle attacks. Organizations should educate their employees about the risks associated with public Wi-Fi and encourage the use of VPNs when connecting to untrusted networks. Assessing mobile device security requires a combination of technical evaluations and user awareness. Employees should be educated about best practices for securing their mobile devices, including the importance of regularly updating operating systems and apps, using strong authentication methods, and being cautious when downloading and installing apps. Additionally, organizations should implement mobile device security policies and procedures to guide employees on safe and secure mobile device usage. Mobile device assessments should also consider the potential risks associated with third-party app stores and app sideloading. Third-party app stores may host malicious apps that can compromise the security of a mobile device. App sideloading, the practice of installing apps from unofficial sources, can also introduce security risks. Organizations should discourage employees from using third-party app stores and sideloading apps onto their devices. Furthermore, assessments should evaluate the organization's ability to remotely manage and secure mobile devices. This includes the ability to locate, lock, and wipe devices in the event of loss or theft. Assessments should also consider the organization's incident response plan for mobile device security incidents. In summary, assessing mobile devices and apps is crucial to ensure the security and privacy of both personal and business data. Mobile device assessments should cover a range of aspects, including physical security, operating system security, app security, network security, and user awareness. By conducting thorough assessments and implementing robust security measures, organizations can mitigate the risks associated with mobile device usage and protect sensitive information from potential threats and attacks.

Evaluating mobile device security is a critical aspect of ensuring the protection of sensitive data and mitigating potential security threats in today's mobile-driven world. Mobile devices, including smartphones and tablets, have become indispensable tools for both personal and professional use, but their widespread adoption has also made them attractive targets for cyberattacks. To assess the security of mobile devices effectively, organizations and individuals must consider various factors that can impact their overall security posture. One of the primary considerations in evaluating mobile device security is the operating system (OS) that powers the device. The choice of OS significantly influences the device's security features, update mechanisms, and overall resilience to threats. For example, Android and iOS are two of the most widely used mobile operating systems, each with its own security model and ecosystem. iOS devices benefit from Apple's tight control over both the hardware and software, resulting in regular security updates and a relatively closed app distribution system. Android, on the other hand, is more open, allowing users to install apps from various sources, which can introduce additional security risks if not managed properly. Evaluators should consider the OS version and whether the device receives timely security updates, as older versions may contain known vulnerabilities that could be exploited. Another crucial aspect of mobile device security evaluation is the device's physical security measures. Physical security includes the protection of the device itself from unauthorized access or tampering. This can involve biometric authentication methods like fingerprint or facial recognition, as well as PIN or password protection. Evaluators should assess the strength and effectiveness of these mechanisms in preventing unauthorized access to the device. Additionally, the presence of hardware-based security features, such as a Trusted Platform Module (TPM), can enhance the device's overall security by providing secure storage and encryption capabilities. Mobile devices often store a wealth of sensitive data, including personal information, photos, emails, and business documents. Therefore, data encryption is a fundamental security feature that should be evaluated. Modern mobile devices typically support full-disk encryption, which protects the data stored on the device by encrypting it with a cryptographic key. Evaluators should verify that encryption is enabled and functioning correctly, as the loss or theft of an unencrypted device can result in data breaches. Mobile app security is another critical consideration when evaluating the security of mobile devices. Apps installed on a device can access various resources, including the camera, microphone, location data, and contacts. Evaluators should assess the permissions requested by each app to determine whether they are appropriate for the app's intended functionality. Excessive permissions or suspicious behavior can indicate potential security risks. Mobile app stores, such as the Apple App Store and Google Play Store, play a role in app security by reviewing and vetting apps before they are made available to users. However, malicious apps can still slip through the screening process. Evaluators should examine the source of apps installed on the device and exercise caution when sideloading apps from unofficial sources. In addition to app permissions, the security of data transmission is crucial. Evaluators should assess whether mobile apps and the device itself use secure communication protocols (e.g., HTTPS) when transmitting sensitive data over networks. The use of unsecured or poorly implemented communication can expose data to interception and eavesdropping. Furthermore, mobile device security evaluations should consider the device's ability to defend against common attack vectors, such as malware and phishing. Evaluators should verify the presence of security software, such as antivirus and antimalware solutions, and assess their effectiveness in detecting and mitigating threats. Phishing awareness and education are essential components of mobile device security, as social engineering attacks can target users through various channels, including emails and text messages. The evaluation should also extend to the device's network security features. Wi-Fi and cellular connectivity are fundamental aspects of mobile device usage, but they can introduce security risks if not configured correctly. Evaluators should assess the device's ability to connect securely to Wi-Fi networks, identify potential risks associated with public Wi-Fi, and ensure that VPN (Virtual Private Network) capabilities are available for secure communication. Mobile devices may also be used for work-related tasks, making them potential vectors for corporate security breaches. Enterprises should evaluate the device's compatibility with mobile device management (MDM) solutions and assess their ability to enforce security policies, monitor device compliance, and remotely wipe or lock devices in case of loss or theft. Finally, it is crucial to consider the human factor in mobile device security evaluations. User awareness and training programs can help individuals understand the importance of device security practices, such as keeping the device and its apps up to date, using strong authentication methods, and being cautious about installing apps or clicking on links from unknown sources. In summary, evaluating mobile device security requires a comprehensive approach that encompasses various aspects of the device, its operating system, apps, and network connectivity. The evaluation should consider physical security measures, data encryption, app permissions, secure communication, defense against malware and phishing, and the human element. By conducting thorough assessments, organizations and individuals can enhance the security of their mobile devices, protect sensitive data, and minimize the risk of security breaches.

Chapter 9: Exploiting Wireless Devices and IoT Vulnerabilities

Identifying vulnerable wireless devices is a crucial step in securing a network against potential threats and vulnerabilities. Wireless devices, including smartphones, laptops, IoT (Internet of Things) devices, and wireless routers, have become integral components of modern life. While they offer convenience and connectivity, they also present security risks that can be exploited by malicious actors. To effectively identify vulnerable wireless devices, it's essential to understand the potential vulnerabilities they may possess. One common vulnerability in wireless devices is outdated or unpatched software. Operating systems and applications on these devices may have known security vulnerabilities that can be exploited by attackers. Identifying devices with outdated software can be achieved through network scanning and vulnerability assessment tools. These tools can detect the version of the operating system and installed applications and compare them to known vulnerabilities. Unpatched or obsolete devices can then be flagged for remediation. Weak or default passwords are another vulnerability that attackers often exploit to gain unauthorized access to wireless devices. Identifying devices with default or weak passwords involves performing password strength assessments. Password cracking tools and techniques can be employed to test the strength of passwords used on these devices. Any devices found with easily guessable or default passwords should be addressed immediately. Many wireless devices, particularly IoT devices, lack proper security configurations, making them susceptible to attacks. Identifying these devices involves examining their network behavior and communication protocols. Anomalous network traffic, unusual ports, or unusual communication patterns can indicate potential security issues. Network monitoring tools can help identify devices that exhibit suspicious behavior. Unencrypted communication is a significant vulnerability, especially for devices that transmit sensitive data. Identifying devices that communicate over unencrypted channels involves packet capture and analysis. By capturing network traffic and inspecting it for encryption protocols (or the lack thereof), vulnerable devices can be located. Unauthorized access points, such as rogue Wi-Fi routers or access points, can introduce security risks to a network. Identifying rogue access points requires active scanning and monitoring of the wireless environment. Wireless intrusion detection systems (WIDS) and wireless intrusion prevention systems (WIPS) can help detect unauthorized access points and their associated devices. Physical security is often overlooked but can be a significant vulnerability. Devices that are physically accessible to unauthorized individuals can be tampered with or stolen. Identifying vulnerable wireless devices in terms of physical security involves assessing the physical access controls in place and implementing measures like locks, alarms, or surveillance cameras. Inventory management and asset tracking are essential for identifying and tracking wireless devices within a network. An accurate inventory of devices, including their make, model, and location, enables organizations to identify and manage vulnerabilities effectively. Asset management systems can help automate this process and maintain an up-to-date record of all wireless devices. Identifying vulnerable wireless devices also requires continuous monitoring and assessment. Security teams should establish a proactive approach to identifying vulnerabilities by conducting regular security audits and assessments. Penetration testing and vulnerability scanning can help uncover vulnerabilities before attackers exploit them. Network segmentation can aid in identifying and isolating vulnerable wireless devices. Segmentation divides a network into separate segments, limiting the potential impact of a compromised device. Security teams can identify vulnerable devices by monitoring network traffic and identifying anomalies within each segment. User education and awareness are crucial for identifying and mitigating vulnerabilities. Teaching users about the risks associated with their wireless devices can lead to better security practices. Users should be encouraged to update their devices regularly, use strong passwords, and report any suspicious activity or unauthorized access. In summary, identifying vulnerable wireless devices is a critical component of network security. Wireless devices pose unique security challenges, including outdated software, weak passwords, insecure configurations, unencrypted communication, rogue access points, physical security risks, and the need for continuous monitoring and assessment. By employing a comprehensive approach that includes vulnerability assessments, active scanning, network monitoring, physical security measures, inventory management, and user education, organizations can effectively identify and mitigate vulnerabilities, strengthening their overall security posture and reducing the risk of security breaches.

Exploiting IoT security flaws has become a common tactic among cybercriminals seeking to compromise interconnected devices. The Internet of Things (IoT) has revolutionized how we interact with technology, allowing everyday objects to connect to the internet and communicate with each other. However, the rapid proliferation of IoT devices has brought about a host of security vulnerabilities that attackers are eager to exploit. Understanding the methods and motivations behind exploiting IoT security flaws is crucial for both device manufacturers and consumers. One primary motivation for exploiting IoT security flaws is gaining unauthorized access to sensitive data. IoT devices often collect and transmit data, such as personal information, health records, or even video footage, making them valuable targets for attackers. Once an attacker gains access to an IoT device, they may intercept or exfiltrate this sensitive data for malicious purposes, such as identity theft or blackmail. Another common motivation is using compromised IoT devices as entry points into larger networks. By infiltrating an IoT device with weak security, an attacker can pivot to other devices or systems connected to the same network. This lateral movement allows them to expand their reach and potentially compromise more valuable targets, such as corporate servers or financial systems. Exploiting IoT security flaws can also be financially motivated. Attackers may seek to control IoT devices to carry out distributed denial of service (DDoS) attacks. Compromised IoT devices can be harnessed to flood a target's network or website with traffic, causing service disruptions and financial losses. These DDoS attacks can be part of extortion schemes, where attackers demand a ransom to stop the attacks. Moreover, some attackers exploit IoT devices for cryptocurrency mining. By infecting IoT devices with mining malware, they can use the device's computational power to mine cryptocurrencies like Bitcoin or Monero, generating revenue for the attacker while slowing down the device's performance. Exploiting IoT security flaws can also lead to privacy violations. IoT devices often have built-in microphones and cameras, and attackers can use these features to eavesdrop on conversations or capture video footage without the user's consent. This invasion of privacy can have serious consequences, especially in settings where personal or confidential information is discussed. Attackers may also exploit IoT devices to gain control over physical systems, such as smart locks, thermostats, or industrial equipment. By compromising these devices, they can manipulate settings, disrupt operations, or even cause physical harm. For example, an attacker could remotely unlock smart door locks to gain unauthorized access to a building or tamper with the settings of an industrial machine, leading to safety hazards. The methods employed for exploiting IoT security flaws vary depending on the vulnerabilities present in the device. One common method is exploiting weak or default passwords. Many IoT devices come with default credentials that users may not change, making them vulnerable to brute-force attacks. Attackers use automated tools to guess usernames and passwords until they gain access. Another method involves exploiting outdated or unpatched firmware. Manufacturers may release security updates to fix vulnerabilities, but users often neglect to apply these updates, leaving their devices exposed. Attackers scan the internet for devices running outdated firmware versions and exploit known vulnerabilities to compromise them. In some cases, attackers take advantage of insecure network configurations. IoT devices may be connected to poorly secured Wi-Fi networks or have open ports that attackers can exploit. Unprotected device-to-device communication can also be intercepted, leading to unauthorized access. Some attackers use social engineering techniques to trick users into disclosing sensitive information or granting permissions. Phishing emails, fake apps, or fraudulent messages can be used to deceive users into providing access to their IoT devices or revealing login credentials. Additionally, malware is a prevalent method for exploiting IoT security flaws. Attackers develop and distribute malware specifically designed to target IoT devices. Once installed, this malware can take control of the device, collect data, or carry out malicious actions on behalf of the attacker. Mitigating the risk of exploiting IoT security flaws requires a collaborative effort from device manufacturers, consumers, and the broader cybersecurity community. Manufacturers must prioritize security in the design and development of IoT devices. This includes implementing strong authentication mechanisms, ensuring regular firmware updates, and conducting security assessments to identify and address vulnerabilities. Consumers play a crucial role by promptly applying security updates, changing default credentials, and being cautious about installing third-party apps or connecting devices to unsecured networks. The cybersecurity community must continue researching and identifying IoT vulnerabilities and sharing this information to raise awareness and facilitate timely fixes. In summary, exploiting IoT security flaws poses significant risks to both individuals and organizations. Attackers are motivated by financial gain, data theft, privacy violations, and the potential for physical harm. Methods for exploiting IoT vulnerabilities range from password attacks to malware distribution and social engineering. Mitigating these risks requires a multifaceted approach that involves manufacturers, consumers, and the broader cybersecurity community working together to improve IoT device security and protect against exploitation.

Chapter 10: Best Practices in Ethical Hacking with Kali Linux NetHunter

Responsible hacking practices, also known as ethical hacking, encompass a set of principles and guidelines that ethical hackers adhere to when conducting security assessments or penetration testing. The primary goal of responsible hacking is to identify and address security vulnerabilities in computer systems, networks, and software applications while avoiding any malicious or harmful activities. Ethical hackers, often referred to as "white hat" hackers, play a crucial role in enhancing cybersecurity by proactively identifying and mitigating potential threats. One fundamental principle of responsible hacking is obtaining proper authorization before conducting any hacking activities. Ethical hackers must have explicit permission from the owner or administrator of the system or network they intend to assess. Unauthorized hacking, even with good intentions, can lead to legal consequences and damage trust within the cybersecurity community. Responsible hackers should always maintain a clear and transparent line of communication with the organization or individual requesting their services. This includes defining the scope of the assessment, outlining the rules of engagement, and establishing a timeline for the testing process. Effective communication ensures that both parties have a shared understanding of the objectives and limitations of the engagement. Furthermore, responsible hacking practices emphasize the importance of respecting privacy and confidentiality. Ethical hackers must handle any sensitive information or data they encounter during an assessment with the utmost care and discretion. This includes safeguarding personal or proprietary data and adhering to relevant data protection and privacy laws. To conduct ethical hacking assessments, responsible hackers often use a combination of open-source and commercial security tools and techniques. These tools help identify vulnerabilities, assess system weaknesses, and analyze network traffic without causing harm or disruption. Responsible hackers should be proficient in the use of these tools and stay up-to-date with the latest advancements in cybersecurity technology. Responsible hacking practices also stress the importance of documenting findings and vulnerabilities. Ethical hackers must maintain detailed records of their assessments, including the methods used, vulnerabilities discovered, and recommended remediation steps. Documentation provides a clear audit trail and allows organizations to prioritize and address identified weaknesses effectively. One crucial aspect of responsible hacking is the principle of "do no harm." Ethical hackers should always exercise caution to avoid causing any damage, data loss, or service disruptions during their assessments. They must conduct their testing in a controlled and non-disruptive manner to minimize any potential impact on the target systems. Responsible hackers should have a thorough understanding of the legal and ethical boundaries of their actions. They must adhere to local and international laws governing hacking activities, intellectual property rights, and data protection. Ethical hackers should never engage in activities that involve stealing, altering, or destroying data, nor should they participate in any activities that are illegal or harmful. Responsible hacking practices emphasize the importance of continuous learning and skill development. The field of cybersecurity is dynamic, and new threats and vulnerabilities emerge regularly. Ethical hackers must stay updated with the latest security trends, vulnerabilities, and attack techniques to effectively assess and protect systems. Maintaining certifications and participating in training programs are essential for ethical hackers to enhance their skills and knowledge. Responsible hacking also involves responsible disclosure of vulnerabilities. When ethical hackers discover security weaknesses, they should follow a responsible disclosure process. This typically involves notifying the organization or vendor responsible for the affected system, providing them with detailed information about the vulnerability, and allowing them a reasonable timeframe to develop and deploy a patch or mitigation. Responsible hackers should avoid publicizing vulnerabilities or exploiting them for personal gain. Lastly, ethical hackers should promote a culture of security and awareness. They can educate organizations and individuals about the importance of cybersecurity and the potential risks associated with vulnerabilities. By raising awareness, ethical hackers contribute to a safer digital environment for everyone. In summary, responsible hacking practices are guided by principles of legality, transparency, privacy, and professionalism. Ethical hackers play a crucial role in identifying and mitigating cybersecurity vulnerabilities while respecting the boundaries of law and ethics. By adhering to these principles and promoting a culture of responsible hacking, ethical hackers contribute to a safer and more secure digital world for all.

Continuing your ethical hacking journey is an ongoing process that involves constant learning, skill development, and staying up-to-date with the evolving landscape of cybersecurity. Ethical hacking is a dynamic field that requires individuals to adapt and expand their knowledge to effectively assess and secure computer systems, networks, and applications. One of the key aspects of advancing in ethical hacking is the pursuit of relevant certifications and qualifications. Certifications like Certified Ethical Hacker (CEH), Certified Information Systems Security Professional (CISSP), and Offensive Security Certified Professional (OSCP) are highly regarded in the industry and can validate your expertise. Earning certifications demonstrates your commitment to ethical hacking and provides tangible proof of your skills to potential employers or clients. In addition to certifications, participating in cybersecurity training programs and workshops can help you gain practical experience and hands-on skills. Many organizations offer training courses that cover various aspects of ethical hacking, from penetration testing to vulnerability assessment. These programs often provide access to specialized tools and environments for real-world practice. Continuous learning is essential in ethical hacking, as cyber threats and attack techniques constantly evolve. Keeping up with the latest trends and vulnerabilities is crucial to staying effective in your role. Reading books, blogs, research papers, and attending cybersecurity conferences can help you stay informed about emerging threats and defensive strategies. Engaging with the cybersecurity community through online forums, social media, and local meetups can provide valuable insights and networking opportunities. Building a personal lab environment is a practical way to experiment with ethical hacking techniques and hone your skills. A lab allows you to test different tools, practice exploitation, and simulate real-world scenarios in a controlled setting. You can set up a lab using virtual machines, physical hardware, or cloud-based resources, depending on your budget and requirements. Participating in Capture The Flag (CTF) competitions is an enjoyable and educational way to challenge yourself and apply your skills. CTF challenges present a wide range of cybersecurity scenarios, from cryptography puzzles to web application vulnerabilities. Competing in CTFs can improve your problem-solving abilities and expose you to new challenges. Networking and collaboration within the ethical hacking community can open doors to opportunities for learning and professional growth. Establishing connections with experienced professionals can lead to mentorship and guidance on your ethical hacking journey. Collaborating on projects or participating in bug bounty programs can provide valuable experience and potentially earn you rewards for identifying security vulnerabilities. As you progress in your ethical hacking career, consider specializing in specific areas of cybersecurity that align with your interests and strengths. Some professionals focus on web application security, while others specialize in network penetration testing or mobile device security. Specialization allows you to deepen your expertise and become a subject matter expert in your chosen field. Developing a strong ethical code is a fundamental aspect of advancing in ethical hacking. Ethical hackers must always adhere to the highest standards of integrity and professionalism. Respecting legal and ethical boundaries, obtaining proper authorization, and maintaining confidentiality are non-negotiable principles. Acting responsibly and ethically is essential to preserving the trust and reputation of the ethical hacking community. Additionally, cultivating problem-solving skills and a hacker mindset is crucial for success in ethical hacking. Effective ethical hackers possess curiosity, persistence, and the ability to think outside the box. They approach challenges with a creative and analytical mindset, seeking innovative ways to identify and exploit vulnerabilities. Ultimately, your ethical hacking journey is a continuous process of growth and development. It requires dedication, a commitment to learning, and a passion for securing digital assets and systems. Ethical hackers play a critical role in safeguarding the digital world from cyber threats, and their contributions are increasingly valuable in our interconnected society. Whether you are just starting or have years of experience, there is always room for growth and improvement in the field of ethical hacking. By staying informed, obtaining certifications, participating in training, building practical skills, networking, specializing, upholding ethical principles, and nurturing a hacker mindset, you can continue your ethical hacking journey and make a positive impact on the cybersecurity landscape.

BOOK 3
AIRCRACK-NG TECHNIQUES
CRACKING WEP/WPA/WPA2 KEYS

ROB BOTWRIGHT

Chapter 1: Introduction to Wi-Fi Encryption and Aircrack-ng

Understanding Wi-Fi encryption protocols is essential for maintaining the security and privacy of wireless networks. Encryption is the process of encoding data to make it unreadable to unauthorized users, ensuring that sensitive information remains confidential. Wi-Fi encryption protocols are designed to protect data transmitted over wireless networks from interception and unauthorized access. One of the earliest and most widely used Wi-Fi encryption protocols is Wired Equivalent Privacy (WEP). WEP was introduced to provide basic security for wireless networks by encrypting data packets sent between devices. However, WEP has several serious security flaws that make it vulnerable to attacks, and it is now considered deprecated and insecure. To address the shortcomings of WEP, Wi-Fi Protected Access (WPA) was developed as a more robust encryption protocol. WPA improved security by using Temporal Key Integrity Protocol (TKIP) to dynamically generate encryption keys for each data session. While WPA was a significant improvement over WEP, it still had some vulnerabilities that could be exploited by attackers. As a result, Wi-Fi Alliance introduced WPA2, which became the standard for Wi-Fi security for many years. WPA2 uses the Advanced Encryption Standard (AES) algorithm to encrypt data and is considered highly secure when configured correctly. However, over time, vulnerabilities and weaknesses have been discovered in WPA2, leading to the development of WPA3, the latest Wi-Fi encryption protocol. WPA3 offers enhanced security features, including stronger encryption, protection against offline dictionary attacks, and improved protection for open networks. One of the key features of WPA3 is the use of the Simultaneous Authentication of Equals (SAE) protocol, also known as Dragonfly, for key exchange. SAE strengthens the security of the initial handshake between a device and a Wi-Fi network, making it more resistant to attacks. Another important aspect of Wi-Fi encryption protocols is the use of pre-shared keys (PSKs) or enterprise authentication. In PSK mode, a Wi-Fi network is protected by a passphrase or key shared among authorized users. While convenient for small home networks, PSKs can be susceptible to brute-force attacks if the passphrase is weak. Enterprise authentication, on the other hand, uses a centralized authentication server, such as RADIUS (Remote Authentication Dial-In User Service), to validate user credentials. This method is more secure and scalable, making it suitable for larger organizations. When choosing a Wi-Fi encryption protocol, it's crucial to consider the level of security required for your network. For most home users, WPA3 with a strong passphrase provides adequate protection against common threats. However, in business or enterprise environments, WPA3-Enterprise with enterprise authentication is recommended for greater security and control. In addition to choosing the right encryption protocol, it's essential to implement other security measures, such as strong network passwords and regular firmware updates for Wi-Fi routers and access points. Furthermore, network segmentation, the use of a virtual private network (VPN), and intrusion detection systems can enhance the overall security of a Wi-Fi network. It's worth noting that Wi-Fi encryption protocols only secure data in transit over the wireless network. End-to-end encryption, such as HTTPS for web traffic and secure messaging apps, is necessary to protect data once it reaches its destination. While Wi-Fi encryption protocols play a crucial role in securing wireless networks, it's also essential to keep them up-to-date. As security researchers discover new vulnerabilities and attack techniques, protocol standards evolve to address these issues. Regularly updating your Wi-Fi equipment and devices to support the latest encryption protocols helps ensure the ongoing security of your wireless network. In summary, understanding Wi-Fi encryption protocols is vital for maintaining the security and privacy of wireless networks. WEP, WPA, WPA2, and WPA3 have evolved to address security weaknesses and provide varying levels of protection. Choosing the appropriate encryption protocol and implementing additional security measures based on your network's requirements is key to safeguarding your wireless communication.

Aircrack-ng is a powerful and versatile suite of security tools primarily used for assessing the security of wireless networks. It is a collection of software utilities designed for monitoring, analyzing, and cracking Wi-Fi networks. Aircrack-ng is widely recognized and utilized within the ethical hacking and cybersecurity communities for various purposes, including penetration testing and vulnerability assessment. One of the primary features of Aircrack-ng is its ability to perform packet capture and analysis on Wi-Fi networks. It allows users to capture data packets transmitted over wireless networks and store them in a capture file for further analysis. Packet capture is a crucial step in understanding the traffic patterns, vulnerabilities, and security weaknesses of a wireless network. Aircrack-ng supports a variety of Wi-Fi adapters, both USB and internal, enabling users to capture packets from a wide range of wireless network interfaces. The captured packets can be saved in standard PCAP format, making it compatible with other network analysis tools like Wireshark. Another essential capability of Aircrack-ng is its ability to perform WEP and WPA/WPA2 key cracking. WEP (Wired Equivalent Privacy) and WPA/WPA2 (Wi-Fi Protected Access) are encryption protocols used to secure wireless networks. However, these protocols may have vulnerabilities that can be exploited to recover the network's encryption keys. Aircrack-ng provides utilities like aircrack-ng and airdecap-ng for conducting WEP and WPA/WPA2 key cracking attacks. The aircrack-ng tool uses captured data packets to attempt to recover the network's pre-shared key or passphrase. Additionally, Aircrack-ng supports dictionary and brute-force attacks to recover WPA/WPA2 passwords. The suite includes tools like aircrack-ng and crunch for generating and testing potential passwords against captured handshakes. Aircrack-ng is capable of conducting both online and offline attacks, making it a valuable tool for assessing the security of Wi-Fi networks. Besides packet capture and key cracking, Aircrack-ng includes tools for various other tasks related to wireless network security. One such tool is airmon-ng, which allows users to put wireless network interfaces into monitor mode. Monitor mode enables the interface to capture all wireless traffic within its range, providing a comprehensive view of nearby Wi-Fi networks and devices. Another tool, aireplay-ng, is used for packet injection, deauthentication attacks, and other techniques to assess network vulnerabilities and test defenses against attacks. Aircrack-ng also includes airbase-ng, which allows users to create rogue access points, aiding in the testing of client device behavior and security configurations. For users interested in analyzing captured network traffic, Aircrack-ng offers airdecloak-ng, a tool that can remove cloaked SSIDs (Service Set Identifiers) from capture files, revealing hidden network names. Furthermore, Aircrack-ng includes a versatile set of utilities for working with EAPOL (Extensible Authentication Protocol over LAN) handshakes, which are essential in WPA/WPA2 key recovery attacks. These tools enable users to extract, convert, and manipulate EAPOL handshake data for further analysis. Aircrack-ng is available for various platforms, including Linux, Windows, and macOS, making it accessible to a wide range of users and systems. The suite is actively maintained and frequently updated to address security vulnerabilities and improve functionality. Users can obtain the latest version of Aircrack-ng from the official website or package repositories of their respective operating systems. In summary, Aircrack-ng is a comprehensive suite of security tools that plays a significant role in wireless network assessment and penetration testing. Its features include packet capture, WEP and WPA/WPA2 key cracking, monitor mode activation, packet injection, rogue access point creation, and EAPOL handshake manipulation. Aircrack-ng is a valuable asset in the toolbox of ethical hackers, cybersecurity professionals, and network administrators for evaluating and securing Wi-Fi networks.

Chapter 2: Preparing Your Environment for Aircrack-ng

Installing Aircrack-ng and its dependencies is a critical first step for those looking to utilize this powerful suite of Wi-Fi security tools. The installation process may vary depending on your operating system, but understanding the prerequisites and following the appropriate steps is essential. Before you begin, ensure that you have a compatible wireless network adapter that supports monitor mode and packet injection. Aircrack-ng's effectiveness relies on the capabilities of your network adapter, so having the right hardware is crucial. The suite is primarily designed for use on Linux-based operating systems, such as Ubuntu, Kali Linux, and Debian. While it's possible to use Aircrack-ng on Windows and macOS, the process can be more complex due to compatibility and driver issues. For Linux users, the installation of Aircrack-ng and its dependencies can be accomplished through package management systems. Open a terminal window and use the appropriate package manager for your distribution to install Aircrack-ng. For instance, on Ubuntu and Debian-based systems, you can use the following command:

bashCopy code
sudo apt-get install aircrack-ng

This command will not only install Aircrack-ng but also fetch any necessary dependencies from the official repositories. For users of Kali Linux, which is a popular distribution for ethical hacking and penetration testing,

Aircrack-ng comes pre-installed. However, keeping the suite updated is essential to access the latest features and improvements. To update Aircrack-ng on Kali Linux, you can use the following command:

```bash
bashCopy code
sudo apt-get update sudo apt-get upgrade
```

The first command updates the list of available packages, while the second one upgrades the installed packages to their latest versions, including Aircrack-ng. If you are using a different Linux distribution, refer to the distribution's documentation or package manager commands for installation. For Windows users, Aircrack-ng can be installed using the Windows Subsystem for Linux (WSL), which allows you to run a Linux distribution alongside your Windows environment. This approach provides a Linux-like environment in which Aircrack-ng can be easily installed and used. To set up WSL and install Aircrack-ng, follow these general steps:
Enable WSL on your Windows system by enabling the feature through Windows Features or by running PowerShell as an administrator and executing the following command:

```powershell
powershellCopy code
wsl --install
```

Choose a Linux distribution from the Microsoft Store, such as Ubuntu, and install it.
Once the Linux distribution is installed, launch it and set up your user account and password.

Open the terminal within the Linux distribution and update the package list by running:

bashCopy code
```
sudo apt-get update
```

Install Aircrack-ng using the following command:

bashCopy code
```
sudo apt-get install aircrack-ng
```

This will install Aircrack-ng and its dependencies within the Linux distribution running in WSL. To launch Aircrack-ng, open the terminal within the Linux distribution and use the suite's command-line tools as needed. For macOS users, Aircrack-ng can also be installed through the use of Homebrew, a package manager for macOS. If you haven't already installed Homebrew, you can do so by following the instructions on the official Homebrew website. Once Homebrew is installed, you can install Aircrack-ng by running the following command:

bashCopy code
```
brew install aircrack-ng
```

Homebrew will take care of downloading and installing Aircrack-ng and its dependencies. With Aircrack-ng and its dependencies successfully installed on your system, you can now start using the suite's tools to assess and secure wireless networks. It's essential to note that ethical hacking activities, including the use of Aircrack-ng, should always be conducted within the bounds of the law and with proper authorization. Unauthorized or malicious use of these tools can lead to legal consequences and harm to individuals or organizations. Always obtain explicit permission from the network owner or administrator before conducting any security assessments or penetration testing. In summary, installing Aircrack-ng and its dependencies is a crucial step for anyone interested in assessing the security of wireless networks. The installation process varies depending on your operating system, but the suite is most commonly used on Linux-based systems. For Windows and macOS users, alternative methods like WSL and Homebrew can provide access to Aircrack-ng's capabilities. Regardless of your platform, ethical and responsible use of Aircrack-ng is paramount, and obtaining proper authorization is a fundamental requirement for conducting any security assessments or testing. By following the installation instructions and adhering to ethical guidelines, you can leverage Aircrack-ng effectively for assessing and securing Wi-Fi networks.

Configuring your wireless adapter is a crucial step in preparing it for use with Aircrack-ng and other network security tools. Your wireless adapter must be set up correctly to operate in monitor mode, which is essential for capturing network traffic and assessing wireless network security. The specific steps and commands required for configuration may vary depending on your operating system and the chipset of your wireless adapter. In Linux-based operating systems, configuring a wireless adapter for monitor mode typically involves using command-line utilities and tools. First, it's important to identify the name of your wireless adapter, which may be displayed as something like "wlan0" or "wlp2s0." You can use the following command to list all available network interfaces and their names:

```bash
iwconfig
```

Once you've identified your wireless adapter's name, you can proceed with configuring it for monitor mode. To do this, you'll need to use the "airmon-ng" utility, which is part of the Aircrack-ng suite. Open a terminal and run the following command, replacing "wlan0" with the name of your wireless adapter:

```bash
sudo airmon-ng start wlan0
```

The "airmon-ng start" command instructs your wireless adapter to enter monitor mode and creates a new interface with the "mon" suffix. For example, if your wireless adapter was named "wlan0," the new monitor mode interface might be named "wlan0mon." You can use the "iwconfig" command again to confirm that the monitor mode interface has been created successfully.

In some cases, you may encounter an error indicating that a process is blocking the creation of the monitor mode interface. This can happen if network management services like NetworkManager are running. To resolve this issue, you can stop the network management service temporarily using the following command:

```bash
sudo service NetworkManager stop
```

After stopping the network management service, you can retry the "airmon-ng start" command to create the monitor mode interface. Once you have successfully configured your wireless adapter for monitor mode, you can use it to capture network traffic, assess wireless network security, and perform various security tests.

On Windows operating systems, configuring a wireless adapter for monitor mode can be more challenging, as not all wireless adapters and drivers support this mode. In some cases, you may need to install custom drivers or use external tools like WinPcap or Npcap to enable monitor mode on your wireless adapter.

To check if your wireless adapter supports monitor mode in Windows, you can use the "Wireshark" packet capture software, which often provides information about available interfaces and their capabilities. Install Wireshark and launch it, then go to the "Capture" menu and select "Options."

In the "Capture Interfaces" window, you should see a list of available network interfaces. Look for your wireless adapter and check if it supports "Monitor Mode" or "Promiscuous Mode." If monitor mode is available, you can select it and start capturing network traffic.

If your wireless adapter does not support monitor mode, you may need to consider using an external USB Wi-Fi adapter that is compatible with monitor mode and Aircrack-ng. These adapters are often recommended for ethical hacking and security testing purposes due to their compatibility and capabilities.

In macOS, configuring a wireless adapter for monitor mode can also be challenging, as macOS has limitations and restrictions on wireless adapter usage. Some external

USB Wi-Fi adapters that are compatible with macOS may support monitor mode, but it's essential to research and verify compatibility before making a purchase.

Overall, configuring your wireless adapter for monitor mode is a critical step in preparing it for use with Aircrack-ng and other network security tools. It allows you to capture network traffic, assess wireless network security, and perform security tests effectively. The specific steps and commands required for configuration may vary depending on your operating system and wireless adapter, so it's essential to consult documentation and resources relevant to your setup. By following the appropriate steps and ensuring that your wireless adapter supports monitor mode, you can leverage Aircrack-ng for effective wireless network security assessments and ethical hacking tasks.

Chapter 3: Cracking WEP Encryption with Aircrack-ng

Cracking WEP (Wired Equivalent Privacy) keys with Aircrack-ng is a common security assessment and penetration testing task. WEP was one of the first encryption protocols used to secure wireless networks, but it is now considered insecure due to vulnerabilities that allow attackers to recover the network's encryption key. Aircrack-ng provides a set of tools and techniques for identifying and exploiting these vulnerabilities to crack WEP keys. Before attempting to crack a WEP key with Aircrack-ng, it's important to understand the basics of how WEP encryption works. WEP uses a shared key mechanism, where both the wireless access point (AP) and the client devices share the same secret key. This key is used to encrypt and decrypt data transmitted over the wireless network. In WEP, the key is typically represented as a series of hexadecimal digits, such as "0A1B2C3D4E." To crack a WEP key, Aircrack-ng relies on a combination of captured data packets and statistical analysis. The process involves capturing a sufficient number of data packets from the target network, as well as a specific type of packet called an "Initialization Vector" (IV). The IV is used to initialize the encryption process and is included in each data packet. Aircrack-ng's tools analyze the captured IVs to identify patterns and statistical anomalies that can be exploited to recover the WEP key. The first step in cracking a WEP key with Aircrack-ng is to put your wireless adapter into monitor mode. This can be achieved using the "airmon-ng" utility, as discussed in the previous section on configuring your wireless adapter. Once your adapter is in monitor mode, you can start capturing data packets from the target WEP-protected network. Aircrack-ng includes a tool called "airodump-ng" that allows you to capture packets from nearby wireless networks. You can specify the target network by its SSID (Service Set Identifier) or BSSID (Basic Service Set Identifier), which uniquely identifies the AP. For example, to capture packets from a network with the SSID "MyNetwork," you can use the following command:

bashCopy code
```
airodump-ng --bssid <BSSID> -c <channel> -w <output_file> <monitor_interface>
```

Replace "<BSSID>" with the BSSID of the target AP, "<channel>" with the channel the AP is using (you can find this information in the output of "airodump-ng"), "<output_file>" with the name of the capture file, and "<monitor_interface>" with the name of your monitor mode interface. Airodump-ng will continuously capture packets and display information about the target network, including the number of data packets and IVs collected.

To expedite the capture process, you can use a technique called packet injection. Aircrack-ng provides a tool called "aireplay-ng" for packet injection, which can generate and inject data packets into the target network. This helps increase the number of IVs captured and speeds up the WEP key cracking process.

Once you have captured a sufficient number of data packets and IVs, you can proceed with the actual WEP key cracking using Aircrack-ng's "aircrack-ng" tool. The tool takes the capture file as input and attempts to recover the WEP key. The command to do this is as follows:

```bash
aircrack-ng -e <SSID> -b <BSSID> <capture_file>
```

Replace "<SSID>" with the SSID of the target network, "<BSSID>" with the BSSID of the target AP, and "<capture_file>" with the name of the capture file. Aircrack-ng will analyze the captured IVs and attempt to recover the WEP key. The success of the cracking process depends on several factors, including the number of IVs captured, the complexity of the WEP key, and the statistical patterns detected by Aircrack-ng.

It's important to note that cracking WEP keys with Aircrack-ng is considered a relatively simple and outdated attack, as WEP is no longer considered secure. Most modern wireless networks use more robust encryption protocols like WPA2 or WPA3. Ethical hackers and security professionals often use WEP key cracking as a learning exercise or to assess the security of legacy systems that may still use WEP.

Additionally, it's essential to conduct such activities only on networks for which you have explicit authorization. Unauthorized access or tampering with wireless networks is illegal and unethical.

In summary, Aircrack-ng provides a set of tools and techniques for cracking WEP keys, an outdated and insecure encryption protocol used in wireless networks. The process involves capturing data packets and IVs from the target network and using statistical analysis to recover the WEP key. While cracking WEP keys with Aircrack-ng is no longer a practical attack against modern networks, it can be a valuable learning experience for ethical hackers and security professionals. Always ensure that you have proper authorization before attempting any security assessments or penetration testing activities.

Troubleshooting WEP (Wired Equivalent Privacy) cracking issues can be a challenging task, but it's essential to understand and address common problems that may arise during the process. WEP encryption is known for its vulnerabilities, and ethical hackers often attempt to crack WEP keys as part of security assessments or penetration testing activities. However, several factors can lead to difficulties or obstacles when attempting to crack WEP keys using tools like Aircrack-ng. Next, we will explore some of the common issues encountered during WEP cracking and provide guidance on troubleshooting and resolving them.

One of the first issues you may encounter when cracking WEP keys is a lack of data packets and Initialization Vectors (IVs) in your capture file. IVs are essential for the cracking process because they contain information that can be analyzed to recover the WEP key. To troubleshoot this issue, you can try the following steps:

Increase Packet Capture: Ensure that you are capturing data packets from the target network continuously. You can use the "airodump-ng" tool to monitor the capture process and confirm that packets and IVs are being collected.

Packet Injection: Use the "aireplay-ng" tool to inject additional data packets into the target network. Packet injection can help generate more IVs and speed up the cracking process.

Change Channel: Some networks may switch channels periodically. If you notice a drop in packet capture activity, it may be because the network has changed channels. Use the "airodump-ng" tool to switch to the correct channel and continue capturing packets.

Another common issue is the slow or unsuccessful recovery of the WEP key even with a sufficient number of IVs. This can happen due to the complexity of the WEP key or because the key is not present in the captured data. To troubleshoot slow or unsuccessful cracking:

Check WEP Key Length: Ensure that you know the correct length of the WEP key you are attempting to crack. WEP keys can be either 64 bits (5 characters) or 128 bits (13 characters) in length.

Verify Key Data in Capture: Examine the captured data packets and IVs to confirm that the WEP key is present. If you cannot find the key data in the capture, it may be necessary to capture additional data or packets.

Complexity of the Key: The complexity of the WEP key, including the use of strong encryption keys or passphrases, can significantly impact the time required for cracking. Ensure that you have the correct key format, and be prepared for the possibility that a highly complex key may take a long time to crack.

Additionally, you may encounter situations where Aircrack-ng reports that the WEP key was found, but the key does not work when attempting to connect to the network. This can happen if the key was incorrectly recovered or if there are issues with the key format. To troubleshoot this issue:

Verify Key Format: Double-check that the WEP key is in the correct format (64-bit or 128-bit) and that it matches the network's configuration.

Reattempt Cracking: In some cases, reattempting the cracking process with the same captured data may yield a different, valid key. Ensure that you are using the correct BSSID and capture file when reattempting.

Use Online Tools: Consider using online WEP key generators to verify the key. These tools can help you generate valid keys based on the information available.

Occasionally, you may experience difficulties in capturing IVs from the target network, even though you are in proximity to the access point. This can occur due to interference, channel congestion, or other wireless network issues. To troubleshoot IV capture problems:

Change Channels: Switching to a less congested or more active channel may increase IV capture. Use the "airodump-ng" tool to monitor nearby networks and choose an appropriate channel.

Proximity to Access Point: Ensure that you are physically close enough to the access point to capture its traffic effectively. Being too far from the AP may result in weak signal strength and limited IV capture.

Monitor Mode Stability: Check the stability of your wireless adapter's monitor mode. Some adapters may drop out of monitor mode or experience issues during prolonged capture sessions. Restarting the adapter or the capture process can help.

Finally, it's essential to remember that WEP cracking is an outdated attack and may not be effective against modern wireless networks using more secure encryption protocols like WPA2 or WPA3. If you encounter persistent difficulties or are unable to crack the WEP key successfully, it may be necessary to consider alternative testing and assessment methods.

In summary, troubleshooting WEP cracking issues can be a complex and sometimes frustrating process, but understanding common challenges and knowing how to address them is essential for ethical hackers and security professionals. Issues such as insufficient IV capture, slow cracking, and invalid keys can be resolved with patience, careful analysis of captured data, and the use of appropriate tools. Additionally, it's crucial to remember that WEP is an outdated and insecure encryption protocol, and modern networks should employ stronger security measures to protect against unauthorized access and attacks. Always conduct ethical hacking activities within the bounds of the law and with proper authorization.

Chapter 4: Cracking WPA and WPA2-Personal with Aircrack-ng

Attacking WPA-Personal networks is a more challenging task compared to cracking WEP keys due to the stronger security provided by the WPA (Wi-Fi Protected Access) protocol. WPA-Personal, also known as WPA-PSK (Pre-Shared Key), relies on a passphrase or pre-shared key (PSK) to encrypt wireless communications. This PSK is used to derive encryption keys dynamically, making it significantly more secure than the static WEP keys. However, determined attackers may still attempt to compromise WPA-Personal networks through various methods. Next, we will explore the techniques and tools used in attacking WPA-Personal networks and discuss the steps involved in conducting such assessments.

One of the primary methods used in attacking WPA-Personal networks is dictionary-based or brute-force attacks on the PSK. In a dictionary-based attack, the attacker uses a list of possible passphrases, also known as a wordlist or dictionary, to attempt to guess the correct PSK. Brute-force attacks, on the other hand, involve systematically trying all possible combinations of characters to find the correct PSK. To perform these attacks, attackers use specialized tools like Aircrack-ng and Hashcat.

To execute a dictionary-based attack on a WPA-Personal network, the attacker typically follows these steps:

Capture Handshake: The attacker captures the WPA handshake, a four-way communication between a client device and the access point during the connection process. The handshake contains essential information needed for the PSK recovery.

Wordlist Preparation: The attacker selects or creates a wordlist that contains potential passphrases. This wordlist may consist of common words, phrases, or character combinations.

Dictionary Attack: The attacker uses a tool like Aircrack-ng to initiate the dictionary attack. The tool iterates through the wordlist, attempting each passphrase against the captured handshake.

Successful PSK Recovery: If the correct passphrase is in the wordlist, the tool will successfully recover the PSK. Once obtained, the attacker can use the PSK to decrypt network traffic and gain unauthorized access to the network.

Brute-force attacks on WPA-Personal networks involve systematically trying all possible character combinations to find the correct PSK. These attacks are more time-consuming and resource-intensive than dictionary-based attacks, but they can be effective if the PSK is sufficiently weak. To execute a brute-force attack, the attacker follows these steps:

Capture Handshake: Similar to the dictionary attack, the attacker captures the WPA handshake.

Brute-Force Setup: The attacker configures a tool like Hashcat to perform the brute-force attack. The tool is configured with the character set, length, and other parameters for generating potential passphrases.

Initiate Attack: The attacker starts the brute-force attack, and the tool begins trying all possible combinations of characters. This process can take a significant amount of time and computational resources.

Successful PSK Recovery: If the correct PSK is within the search space defined by the attacker, the tool will eventually find it. Once recovered, the attacker can use the PSK to gain unauthorized access to the network.

It's important to note that both dictionary-based and brute-force attacks on WPA-Personal networks can be time-consuming and resource-intensive, especially if the passphrase is complex and lengthy. Strong, unique passphrases significantly increase the difficulty of these attacks, making them less practical.

In addition to passphrase attacks, attackers may also employ offline attacks against WPA-Personal networks. These attacks involve capturing the WPA handshake and then attempting to recover the PSK offline using specialized hardware or cloud-based services. Offline attacks can be more efficient and less detectable than online attacks.

To defend against attacks on WPA-Personal networks, network administrators and individuals should follow best practices for passphrase selection:

Use Strong Passphrases: Choose long, complex passphrases that include a mix of uppercase and lowercase letters, numbers, and special characters. Avoid using easily guessable phrases, such as common words or phrases.

Change Passphrases Regularly: Periodically change the WPA-Personal passphrase to reduce the risk of compromise. Regularly updating the passphrase is a good security practice.

Enable WPA3: WPA3, the latest Wi-Fi security protocol, offers stronger security features and protection against offline attacks. If possible, upgrade your network to use WPA3 instead of WPA-Personal.

Implement Network Segmentation: Consider segmenting your network and using different passphrases for different segments. This can limit the impact of a successful attack.

Intrusion Detection: Implement intrusion detection systems (IDS) to monitor network traffic and detect suspicious activities, including repeated failed authentication attempts.

Network Monitoring: Regularly monitor your network for unusual or unauthorized devices connected to it. Network monitoring tools can help identify and respond to potential threats.

Firmware Updates: Keep your router's firmware up to date to ensure that known vulnerabilities are patched.

Attacking WPA-Personal networks is a complex and resource-intensive process, and strong passphrases significantly increase the security of your network. By following best practices for passphrase selection and implementing additional security measures, individuals and organizations can reduce the risk of successful attacks on their wireless networks. It's essential to remain vigilant and proactive in network security to protect against potential threats and unauthorized access. Always conduct ethical hacking activities within the bounds of the law and with proper authorization.

Aircrack-ng is a versatile and powerful toolset commonly used by ethical hackers and security professionals for assessing the security of Wi-Fi networks, including those protected by WPA2-Personal (Wi-Fi Protected Access 2 with a Pre-Shared Key).

WPA2-Personal is a widely adopted security protocol for securing wireless networks and relies on a passphrase, also known as a Pre-Shared Key (PSK), for encryption.

To assess the security of a WPA2-Personal network, attackers often attempt to recover the PSK through various means, and Aircrack-ng provides tools and techniques to facilitate this process.

One of the key elements in attacking a WPA2-Personal network is capturing the WPA handshake.

The WPA handshake is a four-way communication between a client device and the access point during the connection process, and it contains essential information needed for the PSK recovery process.

To capture the handshake, the attacker typically employs a wireless adapter in monitor mode, and tools like "airodump-ng" to scan for nearby networks and capture the handshake when a client device connects or reconnects to the target network.

Once the handshake is captured, it can be used to attempt PSK recovery.

Aircrack-ng offers several methods for recovering the PSK of a WPA2-Personal network, with the primary techniques being dictionary-based attacks and brute-force attacks.

In a dictionary-based attack, the attacker uses a predefined list of potential passphrases, often referred to as a wordlist or dictionary, to attempt to guess the correct PSK.

The dictionary may contain common words, phrases, and character combinations that users commonly use as their Wi-Fi passphrases.

Aircrack-ng's "aircrack-ng" tool is employed in this process, and it iterates through the wordlist, trying each passphrase against the captured handshake.

If the correct passphrase is present in the wordlist, Aircrack-ng successfully recovers the PSK.

However, if the passphrase is complex or unique, it may not be present in the dictionary, making this method less effective.

To address this limitation, attackers may also employ brute-force attacks against WPA2-Personal networks.

Brute-force attacks involve systematically trying all possible combinations of characters to find the correct PSK.

These attacks can be highly resource-intensive and time-consuming, as they require trying a vast number of passphrase combinations.

Tools like Hashcat can be configured for brute-force attacks, with parameters defining the character set, length, and other constraints for generating potential passphrases.

Successful PSK recovery through brute-force attacks is contingent on the complexity and length of the passphrase, as well as the computational resources available to the attacker.

As security measures improve and passphrases become longer and more complex, the feasibility of brute-force attacks diminishes.

It's essential for network administrators and individuals to implement strong, unique passphrases to resist these types of attacks effectively.

In addition to dictionary-based and brute-force attacks, attackers may also employ offline attacks against WPA2-Personal networks.

Offline attacks involve capturing the WPA handshake and then attempting to recover the PSK offline using specialized hardware or cloud-based services.

These attacks can be more efficient and less detectable than online attacks, making them a significant threat.

To defend against attacks on WPA2-Personal networks, network administrators and individuals should follow best practices for passphrase selection.

Choosing long, complex passphrases that include a mix of uppercase and lowercase letters, numbers, and special characters is crucial.

Avoiding easily guessable phrases, such as common words or phrases, can significantly enhance network security.

Regularly changing the WPA2-Personal passphrase is also recommended to reduce the risk of compromise.

Upgrading to more advanced Wi-Fi security protocols like WPA3, if supported by the network equipment, can provide enhanced security and protection against attacks.

Implementing network segmentation and using different passphrases for different segments can limit the impact of a successful attack.

Intrusion detection systems (IDS) should be employed to monitor network traffic and detect suspicious activities, including repeated failed authentication attempts.

Regular network monitoring can help identify and respond to potential threats, while keeping router firmware up to date is essential to patch known vulnerabilities.

Attacking WPA2-Personal networks is a complex endeavor, and strong passphrases significantly increase the security of a network.

By following best practices for passphrase selection and implementing additional security measures, individuals and organizations can reduce the risk of successful attacks on their wireless networks.

Vigilance and proactive network security practices are essential to protect against potential threats and unauthorized access.

It is vital always to conduct ethical hacking activities within the bounds of the law and with proper authorization.

Chapter 5: Aircrack-ng for WPA2-Enterprise and EAP Networks

Cracking WPA2-Enterprise networks poses a more significant challenge than attacking WPA2-Personal networks due to the complex authentication mechanisms and the use of EAP (Extensible Authentication Protocol) methods.

WPA2-Enterprise, also known as WPA2-802.1X, is a robust security protocol commonly used in enterprise environments, educational institutions, and large organizations.

Unlike WPA2-Personal, which relies on a pre-shared key (PSK) or passphrase, WPA2-Enterprise employs a centralized authentication server, typically using RADIUS (Remote Authentication Dial-In User Service) or other authentication servers, for user authentication.

EAP methods, such as EAP-TLS (Transport Layer Security), EAP-PEAP (Protected Extensible Authentication Protocol), and EAP-TTLS (Tunneled Transport Layer Security), are used within WPA2-Enterprise networks to provide strong authentication.

Cracking WPA2-Enterprise networks typically involves capturing the EAP traffic and attempting to recover user credentials or authentication keys.

To crack WPA2-Enterprise networks, attackers often follow these steps:

Capture EAP Traffic: The attacker captures EAP traffic exchanged during the authentication process between the client device and the authentication server.

Dictionary or Brute-Force Attacks: The captured EAP traffic may contain encrypted credentials or authentication keys. Attackers may attempt dictionary-based or brute-force attacks to decrypt this information.

Password Cracking: If user credentials are captured, attackers may try to crack user passwords using offline dictionary or brute-force attacks.

Certificate and Key Recovery: In some cases, attackers may attempt to recover encryption certificates or keys used in EAP-TLS and similar methods. This can be a complex and resource-intensive process.

Cracking WPA2-Enterprise networks is significantly more challenging due to several factors:

Strong Encryption: EAP methods used in WPA2-Enterprise networks typically involve strong encryption and secure authentication mechanisms, making it difficult to intercept and decipher traffic.

Centralized Authentication: The use of a centralized authentication server adds an additional layer of security, making it challenging to obtain user credentials.

Certificate-Based Authentication: EAP-TLS, for example, relies on digital certificates for client authentication, making it even more secure.

Resource Intensive: Cracking EAP-encrypted traffic often requires significant computational resources, including powerful hardware and time.

Legal and Ethical Considerations: Attempting to crack WPA2-Enterprise networks without proper authorization is illegal and unethical, and it can have severe legal consequences.

For legitimate security assessments and penetration testing, organizations should perform authorized testing on their own networks or hire ethical hackers with the necessary skills and authorization to assess the security of their WPA2-Enterprise networks.

To defend against attacks on WPA2-Enterprise networks, organizations can implement several security measures:

Strong Authentication Methods: Use strong EAP methods such as EAP-TLS, which relies on digital certificates for authentication.

Secure Network Configuration: Ensure that RADIUS servers and other authentication infrastructure are securely configured and regularly updated.

Network Monitoring: Employ network monitoring and intrusion detection systems (IDS) to detect unusual or suspicious authentication attempts.

User Education: Educate users about strong password practices and the importance of safeguarding their credentials.

Access Control: Implement strict access control policies to limit network access to authorized users only.

Regular Audits: Conduct regular security audits and assessments to identify and address vulnerabilities in the authentication process.

Cracking WPA2-Enterprise networks is a complex and challenging task that requires specialized skills and resources. Organizations should prioritize security measures to protect against potential attacks and ensure the integrity of their network infrastructure. Ethical hacking and penetration testing conducted within the bounds of the law and with proper authorization can help identify and address vulnerabilities in WPA2-Enterprise networks.

Advanced attacks against enterprise Wi-Fi networks are becoming increasingly sophisticated and pose a significant threat to the security of organizations and their sensitive data.

Enterprise Wi-Fi networks, which often use the WPA2-Enterprise or WPA3-Enterprise security protocols, are designed to provide secure and reliable wireless connectivity for a large number of users.

However, these networks can also be attractive targets for attackers seeking to exploit vulnerabilities and gain unauthorized access.

One advanced attack against enterprise Wi-Fi networks is the Rogue Access Point (AP) attack, where an attacker sets up a malicious AP with a similar name to the legitimate network.

This can trick users into connecting to the rogue AP, allowing the attacker to intercept and manipulate their traffic.

To defend against Rogue AP attacks, organizations can implement Wireless Intrusion Detection Systems (WIDS) that continuously monitor the wireless airspace for unauthorized APs.

Another advanced attack is the Evil Twin attack, where an attacker creates a fake AP that mimics a legitimate one.

This fake AP can capture user credentials and other sensitive information when users unknowingly connect to it.

Defending against Evil Twin attacks involves educating users to verify network names and implement certificate-based authentication methods.

Man-in-the-Middle (MitM) attacks are also a serious concern for enterprise Wi-Fi networks, as attackers can intercept and modify network traffic.

MitM attacks can be especially damaging in environments that handle sensitive information, such as financial institutions or healthcare organizations.

To mitigate MitM attacks, organizations should use strong encryption protocols like WPA3 and implement end-to-end encryption for sensitive data.

Password cracking remains a persistent threat, as weak or reused passwords can be easily exploited by attackers.

Advanced attackers may use sophisticated dictionary attacks, rainbow tables, or even custom-built password-cracking hardware to compromise user accounts.

To counter password cracking, organizations should enforce strong password policies, implement multi-factor authentication, and regularly audit user accounts for suspicious activity.

Enterprise Wi-Fi networks are also susceptible to Denial-of-Service (DoS) attacks, which can disrupt network operations and cause service interruptions.

Attackers may flood the network with excessive traffic or use techniques like deauthentication attacks to disconnect legitimate users. Defending against DoS attacks requires the implementation of intrusion prevention systems (IPS) and network traffic monitoring to detect and mitigate attacks in real-time.

Eavesdropping attacks, where attackers passively monitor network traffic to gather sensitive information, are another advanced threat. These attacks can lead to data leakage, privacy violations, and intellectual property theft.

To prevent eavesdropping, organizations should use strong encryption protocols and regularly update security measures to protect against emerging threats.

Phishing attacks targeting Wi-Fi users are also on the rise, with attackers creating fake captive portals or login pages to steal user credentials.

To combat phishing attacks, organizations should educate users about the risks, use secure authentication methods, and implement content filtering to block known malicious sites.

The use of compromised or infected devices within an organization can lead to insider threats that exploit Wi-Fi vulnerabilities.

These insider threats can be challenging to detect and prevent, making user education and continuous monitoring essential components of a robust security strategy.

Brute-force attacks against Wi-Fi encryption keys are still a viable method for attackers seeking unauthorized access.

While strong encryption protocols like WPA3 offer protection against these attacks, organizations must remain vigilant and proactive in their security practices.

To mitigate the risk of advanced attacks against enterprise Wi-Fi networks, organizations should adopt a multi-layered security approach that includes network segmentation, regular vulnerability assessments, intrusion detection and prevention systems, user training, and ongoing monitoring.

Collaboration with cybersecurity experts and ethical hackers can also help identify and address vulnerabilities before attackers exploit them.

By staying informed about the latest threats and continuously improving their security posture, organizations can better defend their enterprise Wi-Fi networks against advanced attacks and protect their critical assets and data.

Chapter 6: Optimizing Wordlists and Dictionaries

Building effective wordlists is a critical skill for ethical hackers, security professionals, and anyone involved in password cracking or security assessments.

Wordlists are collections of words, phrases, or character combinations used in dictionary attacks and brute-force attacks to guess passwords or passphrases.

The effectiveness of a wordlist can significantly impact the success of these attacks.

One of the fundamental principles of building effective wordlists is understanding the target audience or the user base you are attempting to assess.

Wordlists should be tailored to the characteristics and preferences of the users whose passwords you are trying to guess.

For example, if you are assessing a corporate network, you may include industry-specific terms, company names, and technical jargon that employees are likely to use in their passwords.

In contrast, if you are targeting a gaming community, you might include gaming-related terms, character names, and references to popular titles.

A well-constructed wordlist takes into account the psychology of password creation.

People tend to create passwords that are easy to remember, and this often leads to predictable patterns.

Common password patterns include the use of common words, phrases, dates, and variations of keyboard patterns (e.g., "qwerty" or "12345").

To build effective wordlists, it's essential to include variations of these patterns and commonly used substitutions (e.g., "leet speak" substitutions like replacing "e" with "3" or "o" with "0").

Wordlists should also incorporate information that attackers can gather from publicly available sources.

This may include data from data breaches, leaked password lists, and information about the target's interests or affiliations.

Using known passwords from previous breaches can be particularly effective, as people often reuse passwords across multiple accounts.

Social engineering techniques, such as phishing or pretexting, can also provide valuable insights into potential password choices.

Another strategy for building effective wordlists is to create rulesets that generate password variations systematically.

Rulesets define a set of transformations that can be applied to a base word or phrase to create multiple variations.

For example, a rule might specify that "123" should be appended to the end of every word in the wordlist, creating variations like "password123" and "secure123."

Rulesets can also include transformations like capitalization, character substitutions, and concatenation of words or phrases.

Tools like Hashcat and John the Ripper often support custom rulesets, making it easier to generate a wide range of password variations.

Building effective wordlists can be a time-consuming process, but it's essential to strike a balance between comprehensiveness and efficiency.

A wordlist that is too large may slow down the password-cracking process, while one that is too small may miss potential passwords. One approach to address this is to create multiple wordlists with varying levels of complexity. For example, you could have a small, targeted wordlist focused on common patterns and known passwords, as well as a larger, more comprehensive wordlist that includes a broader range of terms and variations. It's crucial to keep wordlists up to date and continuously expand them to account for new password trends and the evolving linguistic landscape.

Regularly incorporating data from recent breaches and updates from various sources can help maintain the effectiveness of your wordlists.

Collaboration with other security professionals and the cybersecurity community can also be valuable for sharing and improving wordlists.

Ethical hackers and security researchers often exchange wordlists and collaborate on password research projects to enhance their collective knowledge and resources.

In summary, building effective wordlists is a crucial skill for those involved in password cracking and security assessments.

Tailoring wordlists to the target audience, understanding common password patterns, using publicly available information, creating rulesets, and striking a balance between comprehensiveness and efficiency are all key principles in constructing effective wordlists.

Keeping wordlists up to date and collaborating with others in the cybersecurity field can further enhance their effectiveness and contribute to more successful security assessments and password-cracking efforts.

Customizing dictionary attacks is an essential skill for ethical hackers and security professionals when attempting to crack passwords and gain unauthorized access to systems.

Dictionary attacks involve using a list of words, phrases, or character combinations, known as a dictionary or wordlist, to guess passwords or passphrases.

While traditional dictionary attacks involve using pre-built wordlists, customizing dictionary attacks allows attackers to tailor their approach to specific targets or scenarios.

One of the primary advantages of customizing dictionary attacks is the ability to create wordlists that are highly relevant to the target audience.

Rather than relying on generic wordlists, attackers can incorporate words, phrases, and terms that are likely to be used by the individuals they are trying to compromise.

For example, if the target is an organization in the healthcare industry, a customized wordlist might include medical terms, acronyms, and industry-specific jargon.

Similarly, when targeting individuals, attackers may gather information from social media profiles, public records, or other sources to create wordlists that reflect the target's interests, hobbies, and personal information.

Customizing dictionary attacks also involves incorporating variations and common patterns that users often employ when creating passwords.

These variations can include character substitutions, leet speak (e.g., replacing "e" with "3" or "a" with "4"), keyboard patterns (e.g., "12345" or "qwerty"), and combinations of common words.

By creating wordlists that encompass these patterns, attackers increase their chances of successfully guessing passwords.

Another aspect of customizing dictionary attacks is using rulesets to generate password variations systematically.

Rulesets define a set of transformations that can be applied to a base word or phrase to create multiple variations.

For example, a rule might specify that "123" should be appended to the end of every word in the wordlist, resulting in variations like "password123" and "secure123."

Rulesets can also include transformations like capitalization, character substitutions, and concatenation of words or phrases.

Tools like Hashcat and John the Ripper often support custom rulesets, making it easier to generate a wide range of password variations.

Customizing dictionary attacks requires an understanding of the target audience's behavior and preferences when it comes to password creation.

Attackers may conduct research to identify common words and phrases associated with the target organization or individuals.

They may also use techniques like social engineering, phishing, or pretexting to gather information that can be incorporated into their customized wordlists.

It's crucial to note that customizing dictionary attacks should only be carried out in ethical hacking or penetration testing scenarios with proper authorization.

Unauthorized or malicious attempts to guess passwords using customized wordlists are illegal and unethical.

Defending against customized dictionary attacks involves implementing strong password policies, enforcing multi-factor authentication, and educating users about secure password practices.

Using randomly generated, complex passwords that do not follow easily predictable patterns can thwart many dictionary attacks.

Regularly auditing user accounts for weak or compromised passwords can also help organizations identify and rectify potential vulnerabilities.

In summary, customizing dictionary attacks is a powerful technique for ethical hackers and security professionals when attempting to crack passwords and assess system security.

By tailoring wordlists and incorporating variations, patterns, and rulesets that reflect the target audience, attackers can increase their chances of success in penetration testing scenarios.

However, it's essential to emphasize that this skill should only be used within the bounds of ethical hacking and with proper authorization, as unauthorized password-cracking attempts are illegal and unethical.

Defending against such attacks involves implementing robust security measures, strong password policies, and user education to mitigate potential vulnerabilities.

Chapter 7: Capturing Handshakes for Offline Cracking

Handshake capture is a fundamental concept in wireless network security and ethical hacking, serving as a crucial component of various wireless attacks and security assessments.

A handshake capture, also known as a four-way handshake capture, is the process of intercepting and capturing the exchange of cryptographic handshake messages that occurs when a client device connects to a secured Wi-Fi network.

This handshake captures the initial negotiation between the client and the access point (AP), which is essential for establishing a secure connection.

In a typical handshake capture, four specific messages are exchanged between the client and the AP, hence the name "four-way handshake."

These four messages play a vital role in the encryption and decryption of data transmitted over the network.

The first message in the handshake capture is the "Client Hello" message, in which the client initiates the connection by sending a request to the AP.

This message includes information about the supported encryption methods, network SSID (Service Set Identifier), and other essential parameters.

The second message is the "AP Hello" message, which the AP responds with, confirming the selected encryption method and other connection details.

The third message, called the "Group Key Handshake" message, is used to establish a secure group encryption key for broadcast and multicast traffic.

This message ensures that all devices connected to the network can decrypt broadcasted data packets.

The fourth and final message in the handshake capture is the "Client Key Handshake" message, which finalizes the secure connection by confirming the encryption keys with the AP.

Once this exchange is complete, both the client and the AP have the necessary keys to encrypt and decrypt data packets sent between them.

Handshake captures are a valuable tool for both security professionals and attackers.

For ethical hackers and security experts, handshake captures are used for security assessments, vulnerability testing, and penetration testing of wireless networks.

By intercepting and analyzing handshake captures, security professionals can identify weaknesses in a network's security, assess the strength of encryption methods, and determine whether weak or default passwords are in use.

This information can then be used to improve the network's security posture by implementing stronger encryption, enforcing password policies, or addressing other vulnerabilities.

On the other hand, malicious actors may use handshake captures for nefarious purposes, attempting to crack the network's encryption and gain unauthorized access.

One of the most common uses of handshake captures is in password cracking attacks, where attackers use powerful tools like Aircrack-ng or Hashcat to attempt to decipher the captured handshake and recover the network's passphrase.

To protect against unauthorized handshake captures and potential attacks, wireless network administrators should implement several security measures.

First and foremost, using strong encryption protocols like WPA3 is crucial, as these protocols are more resistant to handshake capture and subsequent cracking attempts.

Additionally, organizations should enforce strong and unique passwords for Wi-Fi networks, avoiding easily guessable or default passwords.

Implementing Wi-Fi intrusion detection systems (WIDS) can also help detect and respond to handshake capture attempts in real-time, alerting network administrators to potential threats.

Furthermore, it's essential to monitor and log network activity regularly, allowing for the detection of unusual or suspicious behavior.

In cases where a network has been compromised, changing the network's passphrase and re-establishing a new handshake can prevent attackers from gaining prolonged access.

Overall, understanding handshake capture essentials is vital for both ethical hackers and network administrators to assess and enhance wireless network security.

By mastering this concept, security professionals can better protect their networks against potential threats, while also using it as a valuable tool for assessing and improving security.

Capturing a handshake successfully is a critical skill for ethical hackers and security professionals engaged in wireless network assessments, penetration testing, and vulnerability assessments.

A handshake capture is the process of intercepting and capturing the exchange of cryptographic handshake messages that occur when a client device connects to a secured Wi-Fi network.

These captured handshake messages play a pivotal role in assessing the security of a wireless network.

To achieve a successful handshake capture, there are several tips and best practices that ethical hackers and security experts should keep in mind.

One of the first and foremost considerations is legality and authorization.

Engaging in handshake capture without proper authorization is illegal and unethical, as it involves intercepting network traffic and potentially violating privacy and cybersecurity laws.

Ethical hackers must always obtain explicit permission from the network owner or responsible authority before conducting any handshake capture or wireless assessment.

Furthermore, it is essential to ensure that the assessment is conducted within the boundaries of ethical hacking and in adherence to ethical guidelines.

Another crucial tip for successful handshake capture is selecting the appropriate hardware and tools.

To capture handshakes effectively, a wireless network adapter that supports monitor mode is essential.

Monitor mode allows the adapter to capture all wireless traffic on a specific channel without associating with any access point.

Additionally, the choice of a capture tool is essential, with popular options like Airodump-ng, Wireshark, and tcpdump being commonly used.

Choosing the right tool depends on the specific requirements and objectives of the assessment.

The next step involves identifying the target network.

This may require scanning for nearby wireless networks using tools like Airodump-ng or Kismet to list the available SSIDs, MAC addresses, and associated channels.

Identifying the target network is crucial for focusing the handshake capture efforts on the network of interest.

Once the target network is identified, it's important to determine the most suitable channel for capturing handshakes.

Wireless networks often operate on different channels, and the choice of channel can affect the success of the capture.

Analyze the available channels and select the one that is most actively used by the target network.

Another tip is to consider the capture duration.

Capturing a handshake often requires patience, as it depends on a client device connecting or reconnecting to the network.

In some cases, it may take minutes or even hours for a handshake to occur naturally.

Ethical hackers may need to deploy techniques to deauthenticate or disassociate clients from the network temporarily to trigger a handshake.

However, such actions should be performed with caution and within the scope of the assessment.

Another critical aspect is monitoring the capture progress.

Tools like Airodump-ng provide real-time feedback on captured handshakes, displaying the number of handshakes captured and their associated MAC addresses.

This information can help ethical hackers assess the progress and make adjustments as needed.

Furthermore, optimizing the capture environment is essential.

Eliminating interference and ensuring a stable and strong Wi-Fi signal can significantly improve the chances of capturing a handshake successfully.

Adjust the position of the wireless adapter and antenna for better reception if necessary.

Additionally, understanding the behavior of the target network can be beneficial.

Knowing the network's peak usage times and the likelihood of clients connecting or reconnecting can help time the handshake capture more effectively.

When capturing a handshake, it is essential to avoid unnecessary interference with the network.

Excessive deauthentication or disassociation attempts can disrupt the network and draw attention to the assessment, potentially alerting network administrators or users.

Exercise discretion and consider the impact of your actions on the target network.

Furthermore, ethical hackers should always work towards minimizing their footprint during the assessment.

Once a handshake is captured successfully, it is essential to preserve the integrity of the data.

Store the captured handshake securely and avoid altering or tampering with the data to maintain its authenticity.

Finally, documentation and reporting are vital components of any ethical hacking assessment.

Maintain detailed records of the handshake capture process, including dates, times, tools used, and any relevant observations.

This documentation can serve as evidence and provide valuable insights when presenting findings to the network owner or responsible authority.

In summary, capturing handshakes successfully is a crucial skill for ethical hackers and security professionals.

It requires proper authorization, the right hardware and tools, careful planning, and patience.

By following these tips and best practices, ethical hackers can conduct handshake captures effectively, assess wireless network security, and contribute to enhancing cybersecurity measures.

Chapter 8: Advanced Techniques with Aircrack-ng

Brute-forcing with Aircrack-ng is a technique employed by ethical hackers and security professionals to recover Wi-Fi passwords when other methods, such as dictionary attacks or rainbow tables, prove ineffective.

It involves systematically and exhaustively trying every possible combination of characters to guess the password. This method is a last resort, as it can be time-consuming and resource-intensive, but it can be effective against weak or poorly chosen passwords.

Brute-forcing with Aircrack-ng typically targets Wi-Fi networks secured with the WPA or WPA2 encryption protocols, as these protocols use a more robust four-way handshake process.

The main idea behind brute-forcing is to generate and test potential passwords until the correct one is found.

Aircrack-ng, a powerful open-source tool, can automate this process, making it more efficient and manageable for ethical hackers.

One key factor to consider when employing brute-force attacks is the length and complexity of the password.

Short, simple passwords are more susceptible to brute-force attacks, as they require fewer attempts to guess correctly.

Long, complex passwords with a combination of uppercase and lowercase letters, numbers, and special characters are much more resistant to brute-force attacks. Brute-forcing attempts can be significantly accelerated using powerful hardware, such as high-performance GPUs

(Graphics Processing Units) or dedicated password-cracking machines.

These devices can perform billions of password attempts per second, drastically reducing the time required to find the correct password.

It's important to note that brute-forcing is a time-consuming process, especially for complex passwords.

The time required to crack a password using this method depends on several factors, including the length and complexity of the password, the hardware's processing power, and the available attack resources.

For short and simple passwords, brute-forcing may take only a few minutes or hours, while more complex passwords could require days, weeks, or even months.

Ethical hackers must weigh the potential success of the attack against the time and resources available.

Additionally, when using Aircrack-ng for brute-forcing, it's crucial to have access to a captured handshake from the target network.

The handshake capture contains necessary information, including the encryption keys and cryptographic data, to perform the brute-force attack.

Without a valid handshake capture, the attack is futile.

Once a valid handshake capture is obtained, the next step is to select the appropriate wordlist or character set to use during the brute-force attack.

A wordlist is a predefined list of words, phrases, or character combinations that the attacker wants to test as potential passwords.

There are various wordlists available, ranging from common passwords to custom lists tailored to the target's preferences.

Choosing the right wordlist is essential, as it significantly impacts the success of the attack.

Aircrack-ng allows ethical hackers to specify the wordlist to use in their brute-force attempts.

Additionally, Aircrack-ng can apply rules to the wordlist, allowing for modifications such as capitalization, character substitution, and concatenation.

These rules can help generate variations of the words in the wordlist, increasing the chances of success.

Ethical hackers can also create their own custom wordlists based on information gathered during reconnaissance or social engineering.

These wordlists can include personal information about the target, such as names, birthdays, and other relevant data.

When launching a brute-force attack with Aircrack-ng, it's important to monitor the progress closely.

Aircrack-ng provides real-time feedback on the number of password attempts made and the progress toward finding the correct password.

This information can help ethical hackers assess the effectiveness of the attack and make adjustments as needed.

It's crucial to remain patient during the brute-forcing process, as it may take a considerable amount of time to find the correct password, especially for complex passwords.

In some cases, attackers may need to resort to distributed computing or cloud-based resources to speed up the process.

Furthermore, ethical hackers must always operate within the bounds of ethical hacking and authorized security assessments.

Unauthorized or malicious brute-force attacks are illegal and unethical, and they can result in severe consequences.

Network owners or administrators should be informed of any security assessments or penetration tests, and proper authorization should be obtained.

In summary, brute-forcing with Aircrack-ng is a technique employed by ethical hackers to recover Wi-Fi passwords when other methods prove ineffective.

It involves systematically trying every possible password combination and requires a valid handshake capture from the target network.

Choosing the right wordlist and applying rules can improve the chances of success.

Ethical hackers must operate within the bounds of ethical hacking and obtain proper authorization before conducting any brute-force attacks.

Brute-forcing can be time-consuming and resource-intensive, but it can be an effective method for assessing and improving network security.

In addition to its primary function of cracking Wi-Fi passwords, Aircrack-ng offers several additional features and capabilities that can be valuable to ethical hackers and security professionals.

One of these features is the ability to perform deauthentication attacks, also known as deauth attacks or deauthentications.

Deauthentication attacks involve sending deauth packets to one or more clients connected to a Wi-Fi network, forcing them to disconnect temporarily.

These attacks can be useful for various purposes, including capturing handshakes, testing network security, and assessing the effectiveness of intrusion detection systems.

By deauthenticating clients, ethical hackers can trigger reconnection attempts, potentially leading to the capture of handshake messages required for password cracking.

Aircrack-ng provides a simple command-line interface for performing deauthentication attacks, allowing security professionals to specify the target network and client devices.

Another noteworthy feature of Aircrack-ng is the ability to perform fragmentation attacks.

Fragmentation attacks exploit vulnerabilities in the way some Wi-Fi devices handle fragmented packets.

By sending specially crafted fragmented packets to a target network, attackers can potentially trigger a retransmission of the fragmented packet in an exploitable manner.

These attacks can be used to capture weak IVs (Initialization Vectors) for WEP key cracking or to test the security of specific Wi-Fi devices.

Aircrack-ng includes a fragmentation attack tool, fragtest, that simplifies the process of generating and injecting fragmented packets.

WEP chop-chop attacks are another advanced feature offered by Aircrack-ng.

Chop-chop attacks target WEP-protected Wi-Fi networks by exploiting weak IVs to decrypt encrypted packets.

The attack involves iteratively modifying an encrypted packet's last byte and checking the AP's response to determine if the change was valid.

While this attack is no longer effective against modern, more secure encryption protocols, it serves as an educational tool for understanding Wi-Fi vulnerabilities.

Aircrack-ng provides a tool called chopchop for performing this type of attack.

For those interested in testing the integrity of their own Wi-Fi networks or evaluating the effectiveness of their security measures, Aircrack-ng offers a feature called the "PTW attack."

The PTW (Pyshkin-Tews-Weinmann) attack targets WEP-protected networks by exploiting weak IVs to recover the WEP key.

This attack is more efficient than traditional brute-force methods and can recover the WEP key with fewer captured packets.

Ethical hackers can use the PTW attack to assess the vulnerability of WEP-protected networks and educate network owners about the need for stronger security measures.

In addition to these attack features, Aircrack-ng includes a set of utilities for analyzing and processing captured packet data.

These utilities allow security professionals to examine packet captures, extract relevant information, and perform statistical analysis of wireless network traffic.

One such utility is airtun-ng, which can be used for creating virtual network interfaces, making it possible to capture and inject packets on a specific channel.

Another useful utility is tkiptun-ng, designed for attacking WPA-protected networks that use TKIP (Temporal Key Integrity Protocol) encryption.

TKIP was introduced as a temporary security enhancement for WEP but is no longer considered secure.

Tkiptun-ng attempts to exploit vulnerabilities in TKIP to capture packets and eventually recover the WPA passphrase.

While WPA2 and WPA3 have largely replaced WEP and TKIP for securing Wi-Fi networks, ethical hackers may still encounter legacy networks using these outdated security protocols.

Aircrack-ng's support for legacy encryption methods allows security professionals to assess and educate network owners about the importance of upgrading to more secure options.

Finally, Aircrack-ng offers an integrated wireless network scanner, Airodump-ng, which is an essential tool for reconnaissance and network discovery.

Airodump-ng provides real-time information about nearby Wi-Fi networks, including their SSIDs, MAC addresses, encryption methods, signal strengths, and associated client devices.

Security professionals can use Airodump-ng to identify target networks, gather information about their security, and plan their attacks or security assessments.

In summary, Aircrack-ng is a versatile and powerful tool that extends beyond its primary function of Wi-Fi password cracking.

It offers features for deauthentication attacks, fragmentation attacks, and advanced attacks against legacy encryption protocols.

Additionally, Aircrack-ng provides utilities for analyzing and processing captured packet data, making it a valuable tool for ethical hackers and security professionals engaged in wireless network assessments and penetration testing.

By leveraging these additional features, security experts can gain a deeper understanding of Wi-Fi vulnerabilities and help improve the overall security of wireless networks.

Chapter 9: Cracking WPS (Wi-Fi Protected Setup)

Understanding the vulnerabilities associated with Wi-Fi Protected Setup (WPS) is crucial for ethical hackers and security professionals involved in wireless network assessments and penetration testing.

WPS is a convenient feature designed to simplify the process of connecting devices to Wi-Fi networks by using a Personal Identification Number (PIN) or a physical button on the router.

However, this convenience comes at the cost of security, as WPS implementations have been found to have significant vulnerabilities that can be exploited by attackers.

One of the primary vulnerabilities of WPS is the use of a PIN-based authentication method.

In a standard WPS setup, a user enters an eight-digit PIN into their device, which is then transmitted to the router to establish a connection.

The problem arises from the fact that the eight-digit PIN can be brute-forced by an attacker.

While there are 100 million possible combinations for an eight-digit PIN, some routers have poorly implemented WPS, allowing an attacker to determine whether a part of the PIN is correct.

This drastically reduces the number of attempts required to guess the correct PIN, making it susceptible to brute-force attacks.

Aircrack-ng, along with other tools like Reaver, have been developed to automate the process of brute-forcing WPS PINs.

These tools take advantage of the weaknesses in WPS implementations to quickly discover the correct PIN and gain access to the Wi-Fi network.

Another vulnerability associated with WPS is the lack of lockout mechanisms.

Most WPS implementations do not have mechanisms in place to prevent multiple failed PIN attempts.

This means that attackers can continue to guess PINs without any delay or lockout, further facilitating brute-force attacks.

Additionally, some routers do not implement any delay between PIN attempts, allowing attackers to make rapid, successive guesses.

This lack of security measures makes WPS particularly vulnerable to brute-force attacks.

Furthermore, some routers have vulnerabilities that allow attackers to bypass the need for a PIN entirely.

One such vulnerability is the so-called "Pixie Dust" attack, which exploits weaknesses in the way certain routers generate their cryptographic keys.

By capturing the router's Public Key and part of the Diffie-Hellman exchange, attackers can calculate the Private Key used for encryption, effectively bypassing the need for the PIN.

Tools like Pixiewps and Bully have been developed to automate the Pixie Dust attack.

Ethical hackers and security professionals can use these tools to test the security of routers that are susceptible to this vulnerability.

It's important to note that not all routers are vulnerable to the Pixie Dust attack, and the effectiveness of this attack depends on the specific router's implementation of WPS.

Another critical vulnerability is the use of weak, predictable default PINs by some router manufacturers.

In some cases, routers are shipped with default WPS PINs that are derived from information such as the router's MAC address or serial number.

These default PINs are often well-documented and widely known, making it easy for attackers to guess them and gain unauthorized access to the network.

Furthermore, some routers have vulnerabilities that allow attackers to retrieve the router's default WPS PIN without physical access to the device.

Understanding and exploiting these vulnerabilities is essential for ethical hackers to assess the security of Wi-Fi networks.

To protect against WPS vulnerabilities, network owners and administrators should consider disabling WPS on their routers.

Disabling WPS eliminates the risk associated with PIN-based attacks and brute-force attempts.

Instead, users can rely on traditional methods of connecting devices to the network, such as entering the Wi-Fi passphrase.

Additionally, router manufacturers should focus on improving the security of their WPS implementations by implementing lockout mechanisms, randomizing PIN generation, and addressing vulnerabilities that allow PIN bypass.

Network owners should regularly update their router firmware to ensure that any security patches or improvements are applied.

In summary, understanding the vulnerabilities associated with Wi-Fi Protected Setup (WPS) is crucial for ethical hackers and security professionals.

WPS introduces security risks due to the use of PIN-based authentication, lack of lockout mechanisms, and vulnerabilities in some router implementations.

Tools like Aircrack-ng and Reaver have been developed to exploit these vulnerabilities and automate attacks on WPS.

To protect against WPS vulnerabilities, network owners should consider disabling WPS on their routers and keeping their firmware up to date.

By addressing these vulnerabilities and taking appropriate security measures, network owners can improve the overall security of their Wi-Fi networks.

Exploiting Wi-Fi Protected Setup (WPS) vulnerabilities with Aircrack-ng is a topic of significant interest to ethical hackers and security professionals.

WPS, designed to simplify the process of connecting devices to Wi-Fi networks, has been found to have critical security flaws that can be exploited by attackers.

Aircrack-ng, a powerful open-source tool, provides the means to exploit these vulnerabilities and gain unauthorized access to Wi-Fi networks.

One of the most common methods of exploiting WPS with Aircrack-ng is through a brute-force attack on the WPS PIN.

In a standard WPS setup, a user enters an eight-digit PIN into their device, which is then transmitted to the router to establish a connection.

However, due to poor implementations and the lack of lockout mechanisms, attackers can systematically guess the PIN until they find the correct one.

Aircrack-ng automates this process, making it more efficient and manageable for ethical hackers.

The tool allows users to specify the target network and initiate the WPS PIN brute-force attack.

Aircrack-ng systematically tries all possible combinations of the eight-digit PIN, starting from 00000000 and ending at 99999999.

The tool sends each guessed PIN to the router, attempting to establish a connection.

If the correct PIN is found, the attacker gains access to the Wi-Fi network.

It's important to note that successful PIN-based attacks may take varying amounts of time, depending on factors such as the router's vulnerability and the strength of the PIN.

Some routers have more robust security measures and may have lockout mechanisms that slow down or limit PIN attempts.

However, routers with weak or poorly implemented WPS are more susceptible to these attacks.

Additionally, Aircrack-ng allows users to specify a custom wordlist for WPS PIN brute-forcing.

This feature enables ethical hackers to tailor the attack to the target network, using wordlists that may contain common PINs or patterns associated with the router manufacturer.

By leveraging custom wordlists, attackers can increase the chances of finding the correct PIN more quickly.

Furthermore, Aircrack-ng provides options for fine-tuning the brute-force attack, such as setting a maximum number of attempts or specifying a range of PINs to test.

Ethical hackers can use these options to optimize their WPS PIN exploitation efforts.

In addition to brute-forcing the WPS PIN, Aircrack-ng also includes the Reaver tool, which is specifically designed for exploiting WPS vulnerabilities.

Reaver automates the process of attacking the WPS protocol by sending a series of requests to the router, attempting to retrieve the WPS PIN and recover the Wi-Fi passphrase.

Reaver is known for its speed and effectiveness in exploiting WPS vulnerabilities, making it a popular choice for ethical hackers engaged in Wi-Fi penetration testing.

When using Aircrack-ng or Reaver to exploit WPS vulnerabilities, it's essential to have physical proximity to the target network.

WPS attacks require the attacker to be within range of the Wi-Fi network, as they need to communicate directly with the router.

Additionally, attackers must be prepared for the potential consequences of their actions, as unauthorized access to computer networks is illegal and unethical.

Performing WPS attacks without proper authorization is a violation of computer crime laws in many jurisdictions.

Ethical hackers and security professionals should always obtain permission from network owners or administrators before conducting any penetration testing or security assessments.

Moreover, it's essential to use these tools responsibly and in controlled environments to prevent unintended consequences.

In summary, exploiting WPS vulnerabilities with Aircrack-ng is a technique that can be employed by ethical hackers and security professionals to assess the security of Wi-Fi networks.

WPS, designed for user convenience, introduces significant security risks due to its vulnerabilities, including weak PINs and the lack of lockout mechanisms.

Aircrack-ng and Reaver provide tools for automating the exploitation of WPS weaknesses, allowing users to test the security of their networks and educate network owners about the risks.

However, ethical hackers must always operate within the boundaries of legal and ethical standards, obtaining proper authorization before conducting any penetration testing or security assessments.

Chapter 10: Mitigating Aircrack-ng Attacks and Defending Your Network

Protecting your Wi-Fi network is of paramount importance in today's interconnected world where wireless networks are ubiquitous and constantly under threat from malicious actors.

Your Wi-Fi network is the gateway to the internet for your devices, and securing it is essential to safeguard your sensitive data, maintain your privacy, and prevent unauthorized access.

To protect your Wi-Fi network effectively, you should start by changing the default login credentials for your router.

Many routers come with default usernames and passwords that are well-known and often exploited by attackers.

Changing these credentials to strong and unique values is the first line of defense against unauthorized access to your router's settings.

It's also crucial to keep your router's firmware up to date, as manufacturers regularly release updates that address security vulnerabilities and improve overall network security.

Outdated firmware can leave your network exposed to known threats, so it's essential to check for updates regularly and install them promptly.

In addition to updating your router's firmware, it's advisable to disable any unnecessary services and features that you don't use.

Routers often come with features like remote management or WPS, which, if not needed, should be turned off to reduce potential attack surfaces.

Another critical aspect of protecting your Wi-Fi network is configuring strong encryption.

Use WPA3 (Wi-Fi Protected Access 3) or, if not available, WPA2 encryption with a strong passphrase that combines uppercase and lowercase letters, numbers, and special characters.

Avoid using easily guessable passphrases like common words or phrases and opt for something unique and complex.

Furthermore, consider changing your Wi-Fi network's default SSID (Service Set Identifier), which is the network's name.

Leaving it as the default, which often includes the router's manufacturer name, makes it easier for attackers to identify the type of router you're using.

Choose a custom SSID that doesn't reveal any information about your router or location.

Enabling MAC (Media Access Control) address filtering can add an extra layer of security to your Wi-Fi network.

With MAC address filtering, only devices with approved MAC addresses can connect to your network.

While this method is not foolproof (MAC addresses can be spoofed), it can help deter casual attackers.

To protect against unauthorized access attempts, consider setting up an intrusion detection system (IDS) or intrusion prevention system (IPS) for your Wi-Fi network.

These systems can monitor network traffic for suspicious activity and block or alert you to potential threats.

Regularly review the logs and alerts generated by your IDS/IPS to stay informed about any security incidents on your network.

Another important aspect of network protection is the use of strong and unique passwords for all devices and accounts connected to your network.

This includes not only your router's login credentials but also the passwords for your computers, smartphones, and any IoT (Internet of Things) devices.

Using a password manager can help you generate, store, and manage complex passwords for all your accounts.

When setting up your Wi-Fi network, it's essential to segment it into multiple networks or VLANs (Virtual LANs) if your router supports this feature.

Segmentation can help isolate different types of devices (e.g., guest devices, IoT devices, and personal devices) from each other to limit potential attack vectors.

For example, if an IoT device were compromised, segmenting the network could prevent the attacker from easily accessing your personal devices.

Always change default credentials on IoT devices and keep their firmware up to date, as these devices are often targeted by attackers.

Consider using a separate guest network for visitors, which provides internet access but restricts access to your main network and devices.

This helps protect your sensitive data while allowing guests to use your Wi-Fi.

If your router supports it, enable a firewall to filter incoming and outgoing network traffic.

A firewall can block malicious traffic and prevent unauthorized access to your network.

Additionally, regularly review and update the firewall rules to ensure they align with your network's security requirements.

To enhance security further, it's a good practice to disable remote administration for your router.

Remote administration allows you to manage your router's settings from outside your network, but it also presents a potential security risk if not properly secured.

Unless you have a specific need for remote access, it's best to disable this feature to reduce the attack surface.

Regularly monitoring your network for unusual activity is crucial for early threat detection.

Consider using network monitoring tools that can alert you to potential security issues, such as unexpected device connections or unusual traffic patterns.

Lastly, educate yourself and your family members about online security best practices.

Teach them about the importance of strong passwords, not clicking on suspicious links or downloading files from unknown sources, and being cautious when sharing personal information online.

Creating a security-aware culture in your home can go a long way in protecting your Wi-Fi network and personal data.

In summary, protecting your Wi-Fi network is a multi-faceted endeavor that involves a combination of secure configurations, regular updates, strong passwords, and vigilance.

By following these best practices and staying informed about emerging threats, you can significantly reduce the risk of security breaches and ensure the safety of your wireless network and connected devices.

Identifying and responding to Aircrack-ng attacks is a critical skill for network administrators and security professionals.

Aircrack-ng is a powerful tool used by ethical hackers for testing and securing Wi-Fi networks, but it can also be exploited by malicious individuals for unauthorized access. Recognizing the signs of Aircrack-ng attacks is the first step in protecting your network.

One common indicator of an Aircrack-ng attack is a sudden increase in network traffic, particularly in the form of deauthentication or disassociation packets.

Aircrack-ng uses these packets to forcibly disconnect devices from the network, making it easier to capture handshake packets for subsequent cracking attempts.

If you notice a significant spike in such packets on your network, it could be a sign of an ongoing Aircrack-ng attack.

Another telltale sign of an Aircrack-ng attack is the presence of excessive failed authentication attempts in your network logs.

Attackers using Aircrack-ng often attempt to crack Wi-Fi passwords by repeatedly guessing them.

This results in multiple failed authentication attempts, which can be logged by your network's security systems.

If you observe an unusually high number of failed authentication attempts, it may indicate an Aircrack-ng attack in progress.

Furthermore, monitor your network for unusual or unauthorized devices attempting to connect.

Aircrack-ng attackers need to be within range of your Wi-Fi network to capture handshake packets, so they might be physically close to your location.

If you notice unknown devices attempting to connect to your network, it's a potential red flag.

To respond effectively to Aircrack-ng attacks, it's crucial to have a well-defined incident response plan in place.

The first step in your response plan should be to isolate the compromised network segment.

This can be achieved by disabling the compromised access point, either physically or through remote management if possible.

Isolating the affected segment can prevent further unauthorized access and protect other parts of your network.

Next, identify the source of the attack by reviewing network logs, traffic patterns, and device authentication records.

Look for any suspicious or anomalous behavior that may point to the attacker's location or methods.

Once you have identified the source of the attack, consider involving law enforcement if necessary.

Unauthorized network access is a potential crime, and law enforcement agencies may be able to assist in tracking down and apprehending the attacker.

In parallel, change the Wi-Fi network's password and encryption key to prevent further unauthorized access.

Choose a strong and complex passphrase to enhance security, and ensure that all connected devices are updated with the new credentials.

Additionally, update the firmware of your Wi-Fi router to the latest version to patch any known vulnerabilities.

As part of your response, assess the security of your network to identify weaknesses that may have been exploited by the attacker.

Conduct a thorough security audit, review firewall rules, and check for any open ports or services that could be leveraged in future attacks.

Implement any necessary security improvements to fortify your network against similar threats.

Finally, educate your network users about the incident and the importance of practicing good cybersecurity hygiene.

Remind them of the risks associated with weak passwords and the importance of not sharing network access credentials with unauthorized individuals.

Encourage the use of strong, unique passwords and two-factor authentication where applicable.

By taking these steps and remaining vigilant, you can identify and respond to Aircrack-ng attacks effectively, mitigate potential damage, and enhance the security of your Wi-Fi network.

BOOK 4
KISMET AND WIRESHARK
ADVANCED WIRELESS NETWORK ANALYSIS

ROB BOTWRIGHT

Chapter 1: Introduction to Advanced Wireless Network Analysis

The importance of advanced wireless analysis cannot be overstated in today's increasingly interconnected world.

As wireless technology continues to evolve and become integral to our daily lives, understanding and effectively analyzing wireless networks have become crucial for various purposes.

One of the primary reasons for the importance of advanced wireless analysis is the critical role that wireless networks play in modern communications.

From home Wi-Fi networks to large-scale corporate infrastructures, wireless technology underpins the connectivity of countless devices, making it essential to ensure the reliability and security of these networks.

Advanced wireless analysis provides the means to assess the performance, security, and integrity of wireless networks, helping both individuals and organizations maintain their connectivity and protect their data.

Wireless analysis tools and techniques have evolved significantly in recent years, enabling professionals to gain deeper insights into network behavior and potential vulnerabilities.

These advanced capabilities empower network administrators, security experts, and ethical hackers to identify and address issues proactively.

Moreover, advanced wireless analysis is essential for troubleshooting network performance problems.

Wireless networks can experience a range of issues, including signal interference, coverage gaps, and bandwidth limitations.

Through advanced analysis, network administrators can pinpoint the root causes of these problems and take corrective actions, ensuring optimal network performance.

Additionally, wireless analysis is vital for identifying and mitigating security threats.

As the number of wireless devices and networks grows, so does the potential for cyberattacks and unauthorized access.

Advanced analysis tools can detect unusual network behavior, unauthorized devices, and potential vulnerabilities that might be exploited by attackers.

This proactive approach to security helps organizations safeguard their sensitive data and maintain the confidentiality, integrity, and availability of their networks.

Furthermore, advanced wireless analysis is invaluable for optimizing network design and capacity planning.

As organizations expand and adopt new technologies, they must ensure that their wireless infrastructure can handle the increased demand for connectivity.

Advanced analysis tools can simulate network scenarios, predict traffic patterns, and recommend improvements to enhance network capacity and coverage.

This proactive approach to network management helps organizations avoid performance bottlenecks and downtime.

Another crucial aspect of advanced wireless analysis is its role in compliance and regulatory requirements.

Certain industries, such as healthcare and finance, have strict regulations governing the security and privacy of wireless networks.

Advanced analysis tools can assist organizations in demonstrating compliance with these regulations by identifying and addressing security weaknesses and vulnerabilities.

Moreover, wireless analysis is indispensable in the realm of wireless penetration testing and ethical hacking.

Ethical hackers use advanced tools and techniques to assess the security of wireless networks and identify potential weaknesses that could be exploited by malicious actors.

By conducting thorough wireless analysis, ethical hackers can help organizations fortify their defenses and protect against real-world cyber threats.

In the context of advanced wireless analysis, technologies like Wireshark and Kismet are instrumental.

Wireshark, for instance, is a popular open-source packet analyzer that allows users to capture and inspect data packets traveling over a wireless network.

With Wireshark, network professionals can delve deep into network traffic, analyze protocol behavior, and troubleshoot network issues effectively.

Kismet, on the other hand, is a versatile wireless network detector, sniffer, and intrusion detection system.

It can discover hidden wireless networks, detect rogue access points, and monitor network traffic for suspicious activity.

These tools, along with others, form the foundation of advanced wireless analysis, equipping professionals with the capabilities needed to manage, secure, and optimize wireless networks.

In summary, the importance of advanced wireless analysis cannot be overstated in today's interconnected world.

Wireless technology is ubiquitous, and the integrity and security of wireless networks are critical for individuals and organizations alike.

Advanced analysis tools and techniques empower professionals to assess network performance, troubleshoot issues, detect security threats, and plan for network growth.

Moreover, they play a vital role in compliance, ethical hacking, and ensuring the reliability and security of wireless networks in an ever-evolving technological landscape.

In the realm of advanced analysis, several key tools and concepts play a pivotal role in gaining deeper insights into complex systems and networks.

These tools and concepts are indispensable for professionals seeking to understand, troubleshoot, and optimize various aspects of technology and infrastructure.

One of the fundamental concepts in advanced analysis is data mining, which involves the process of discovering patterns, trends, and insights from large datasets.

Data mining tools, such as machine learning algorithms, enable analysts to extract valuable information from vast amounts of data.

These insights can be applied in various domains, from predicting consumer behavior to identifying network anomalies.

Network monitoring and analysis tools are also essential for advanced analysis, allowing professionals to observe and evaluate the performance and behavior of computer networks.

Tools like Wireshark, Nagios, and PRTG Network Monitor provide real-time visibility into network traffic, device status, and application performance.

By closely monitoring network activity, professionals can detect issues, optimize network performance, and enhance security.

Intrusion detection and prevention systems (IDPS) are critical tools for identifying and mitigating security threats in real-time.

These systems monitor network traffic and behavior, looking for signs of malicious activity or policy violations.

When suspicious behavior is detected, an IDPS can take immediate action to block the threat or alert security personnel.

Advanced analysis also relies heavily on the use of performance monitoring tools.

These tools help professionals assess the efficiency and effectiveness of systems, applications, and services.

Performance monitoring tools collect data on resource utilization, response times, and other key metrics, enabling organizations to fine-tune their infrastructure for optimal performance.

Furthermore, log analysis tools are indispensable for advanced analysis, as they allow professionals to review and analyze logs generated by various systems and applications.

Log analysis tools can help uncover trends, anomalies, and security incidents by aggregating and parsing log data from diverse sources.

Moreover, advanced analysis often involves the use of visualization tools to represent complex data in a more understandable and actionable format.

Visualization tools, such as Tableau and Power BI, enable analysts to create interactive charts, graphs, and dashboards that provide insights at a glance.

These visualizations can aid in decision-making, trend analysis, and data exploration.

When conducting advanced analysis, professionals frequently employ statistical analysis techniques to uncover meaningful patterns and relationships within data.

Statistical tools, like R and Python with libraries such as Pandas and NumPy, allow analysts to perform hypothesis testing, regression analysis, and other statistical tests.

These techniques can provide valuable insights into the behavior of systems, processes, and phenomena.

Machine learning, a subset of artificial intelligence, plays a vital role in advanced analysis.

Machine learning algorithms can automatically learn and adapt to data, making them valuable for tasks such as predictive modeling, anomaly detection, and pattern recognition.

These algorithms can be trained to identify complex patterns and trends that may be difficult to discern through traditional analysis methods.

In the realm of network security, threat intelligence tools and services are essential for staying informed about the latest cyber threats and vulnerabilities.

These tools collect and analyze threat data from various sources, including malware samples, hacker forums, and security feeds.

By leveraging threat intelligence, organizations can proactively defend against emerging threats.

Intrusion detection and prevention systems (IDPS) are critical tools for identifying and mitigating security threats in real-time.

These systems monitor network traffic and behavior, looking for signs of malicious activity or policy violations.

When suspicious behavior is detected, an IDPS can take immediate action to block the threat or alert security personnel.

Advanced analysis also relies heavily on the use of performance monitoring tools.

These tools help professionals assess the efficiency and effectiveness of systems, applications, and services.

Performance monitoring tools collect data on resource utilization, response times, and other key metrics, enabling organizations to fine-tune their infrastructure for optimal performance.

Furthermore, log analysis tools are indispensable for advanced analysis, as they allow professionals to review and analyze logs generated by various systems and applications.

Log analysis tools can help uncover trends, anomalies, and security incidents by aggregating and parsing log data from diverse sources.

Moreover, advanced analysis often involves the use of visualization tools to represent complex data in a more understandable and actionable format.

Visualization tools, such as Tableau and Power BI, enable analysts to create interactive charts, graphs, and dashboards that provide insights at a glance.

These visualizations can aid in decision-making, trend analysis, and data exploration.

When conducting advanced analysis, professionals frequently employ statistical analysis techniques to uncover meaningful patterns and relationships within data.

Statistical tools, like R and Python with libraries such as Pandas and NumPy, allow analysts to perform hypothesis testing, regression analysis, and other statistical tests.

These techniques can provide valuable insights into the behavior of systems, processes, and phenomena.

Machine learning, a subset of artificial intelligence, plays a vital role in advanced analysis.

Machine learning algorithms can automatically learn and adapt to data, making them valuable for tasks such as predictive modeling, anomaly detection, and pattern recognition.

These algorithms can be trained to identify complex patterns and trends that may be difficult to discern through traditional analysis methods.

In the realm of network security, threat intelligence tools and services are essential for staying informed about the latest cyber threats and vulnerabilities.

These tools collect and analyze threat data from various sources, including malware samples, hacker forums, and security feeds.

By leveraging threat intelligence, organizations can proactively defend against emerging threats.

Chapter 2: Setting Up Kismet and Wireshark for Advanced Analysis

Installing and configuring Kismet, a powerful wireless network detection and analysis tool, is an essential step for professionals looking to conduct advanced wireless analysis.

Kismet is an open-source tool that is widely used for monitoring and analyzing wireless networks, making it an indispensable part of the toolkit for network administrators, security experts, and ethical hackers.

To begin the installation process, it's important to ensure that your system meets the necessary requirements.

Kismet is available for various platforms, including Linux, macOS, and Windows, so you should choose the appropriate version for your operating system.

Once you have determined the compatibility of your system, you can proceed with the installation.

For Linux users, Kismet can often be installed using package managers like APT for Debian-based distributions or YUM for Red Hat-based distributions.

The installation command may vary depending on your Linux distribution, so it's essential to refer to the official Kismet documentation or the package manager's documentation for guidance.

For macOS users, Kismet can be installed using the Homebrew package manager, which simplifies the installation process.

You can use the following command to install Kismet on macOS:

Copy code

brew install kismet

Windows users have the option of using the Kismet Windows installer, which provides an easy-to-use graphical interface for installation.

After successfully installing Kismet, the next step is to configure it to suit your specific needs.

Kismet's configuration file, typically located at /etc/kismet/kismet.conf on Linux systems, allows you to customize various aspects of the tool's behavior.

To edit the configuration file, you can use a text editor of your choice, such as Vim, Nano, or Gedit.

Within the configuration file, you'll find a plethora of options that you can modify to tailor Kismet to your requirements.

For example, you can specify the wireless network interfaces that Kismet should monitor by configuring the "source" section in the configuration file.

You can also set the storage location for captured data, configure data logging options, and define how Kismet should handle alerts and notifications.

Kismet offers extensive flexibility, allowing you to fine-tune its behavior to meet your specific objectives.

One important configuration aspect is defining the channels and frequency bands you want Kismet to monitor.

This ensures that Kismet captures data from the desired wireless networks and channels.

Additionally, you can configure the data capture format, specifying whether you want to save captured data in the PCAP format or other formats supported by Kismet.

Furthermore, Kismet supports the use of plugins, which can extend its functionality.

These plugins can be configured within the Kismet configuration file, and they offer additional features and capabilities.

For example, you can use plugins to integrate Kismet with external tools for more advanced analysis or data processing.

Once you have customized the Kismet configuration to your liking, it's time to start the Kismet server and begin monitoring wireless networks.

You can start the Kismet server by running the following command:

Copy code

kismet_server

This command initiates the Kismet server, which will begin scanning and collecting data from nearby wireless networks.

Kismet's user interface can be accessed through a web browser, making it convenient to monitor and analyze wireless network activity.

To access the web interface, open your preferred web browser and navigate to the following URL:

arduinoCopy code

http://localhost:2501

This URL will display the Kismet web interface, providing you with real-time information about detected wireless networks, devices, and network traffic.

The web interface offers a range of features, including interactive maps, detailed network information, and advanced filtering options.

You can use these features to explore wireless networks in your vicinity, identify rogue access points, and analyze network traffic patterns.

In addition to the web interface, Kismet also provides a command-line interface (CLI) for users who prefer working in a terminal environment.

The CLI offers various commands and options for controlling Kismet's behavior, viewing collected data, and managing configurations.

Kismet's versatility and ease of use make it a valuable tool for a wide range of wireless analysis tasks.

Whether you are interested in monitoring your own Wi-Fi network for security purposes or conducting in-depth wireless penetration testing, Kismet provides the necessary capabilities and flexibility.

Furthermore, Kismet's active development community ensures that the tool is regularly updated with new features and improvements, making it a reliable choice for professionals in the field of wireless network analysis.

In summary, installing and configuring Kismet is a crucial step for professionals seeking to conduct advanced wireless analysis.

Kismet's flexibility, extensive configuration options, and user-friendly web interface make it a powerful tool for monitoring and analyzing wireless networks.

By following the installation and configuration steps outlined Next, you can harness the capabilities of Kismet to gain valuable insights into wireless network behavior and security.

Configuring Wireshark, a widely-used network protocol analyzer, for advanced analysis is an essential skill for professionals in the field of network security, administration, and troubleshooting.

Wireshark, formerly known as Ethereal, is an open-source tool that allows users to capture and inspect data packets on a network.

Its versatility and extensive feature set make it a valuable resource for examining network traffic, identifying issues, and enhancing security.

Before diving into the configuration of Wireshark, it's important to ensure that you have the software installed on your system.

Wireshark is available for various platforms, including Windows, macOS, and Linux, and can be downloaded from the official website.

Once installed, you can launch Wireshark to begin capturing and analyzing network traffic.

Before capturing packets, it's essential to select the appropriate network interface to monitor.

Wireshark allows you to choose from a list of available network interfaces, such as Ethernet adapters, Wi-Fi cards, or virtual interfaces.

Selecting the correct interface ensures that you capture traffic relevant to your analysis.

After selecting the interface, you can start capturing packets by clicking the "Start" button in the Wireshark interface.

However, before diving into packet capture, it's wise to configure Wireshark to capture only the data you need.

One way to do this is by applying display filters, which allow you to focus on specific types of traffic or packets that match specific criteria.

Display filters can be applied in the "Display Filter" field at the top of the Wireshark window, and they help reduce the volume of captured data.

Wireshark provides a vast array of display filter options, allowing you to filter by source or destination IP address, port number, protocol, or even specific packet content.

By using display filters effectively, you can narrow down your analysis to the packets of interest and avoid overwhelming yourself with irrelevant data.

Additionally, Wireshark offers the option to set up capture filters, which determine which packets are recorded during the capture process.

Capture filters are applied at a lower level than display filters and can significantly reduce the amount of data captured, especially in high-traffic environments.

To create a capture filter, you can go to "Capture" > "Capture Filters" and define your filter criteria using the Berkeley Packet Filter (BPF) syntax.

For example, you can set a capture filter to only capture HTTP traffic or packets from a specific IP address.

Another essential aspect of configuring Wireshark for advanced analysis is the use of profiles.

Profiles in Wireshark allow you to save and load custom configurations, including display filters, capture filters, and preferences.

By creating and utilizing profiles, you can streamline your workflow and switch between different analysis scenarios with ease.

For instance, you might have a profile for monitoring VoIP traffic, another for troubleshooting DNS issues, and yet another for analyzing web traffic.

Each profile can have its specific settings and filters tailored to the task at hand.

Additionally, Wireshark supports the creation of coloring rules, which help visually identify packets of interest based on specific criteria.

Coloring rules can be configured in the "View" menu under "Coloring Rules."

You can define rules that highlight packets with specific characteristics, such as error flags or specific protocol behavior.

This visual aid can make it easier to spot anomalies or patterns in your network traffic.

Furthermore, Wireshark provides the option to create custom columns in the packet list pane, allowing you to display additional information about captured packets.

Custom columns can be configured through the "Edit" menu under "Preferences" and can include details like packet length, timestamp, or custom protocol-specific information.

Tailoring the columns to your analysis needs can enhance your ability to quickly identify relevant packets.

To further refine your analysis, you can use Wireshark's expert system, which evaluates packets for potential issues and displays warnings or errors in the "Expert Info" section of the packet details pane.

The expert system categorizes issues into various severity levels, helping you prioritize your troubleshooting efforts.

Additionally, Wireshark supports the creation of profiles for experts, allowing you to enable or disable specific expert information categories based on your analysis requirements.

This fine-grained control ensures that you focus on the most critical aspects of your network traffic.

For professionals conducting advanced analysis, the use of statistics and protocol analysis is crucial.

Wireshark offers comprehensive statistics options, including protocol hierarchy statistics, endpoint statistics, and flow statistics.

These statistics can provide insights into network utilization, top talkers, or protocol distribution, helping you identify unusual patterns or performance bottlenecks.

Furthermore, Wireshark's protocol analysis capabilities enable you to dive deep into specific protocols, such as TCP, HTTP, or DNS.

You can dissect protocol fields, examine protocol-specific behaviors, and track conversations between network entities.

Understanding the intricacies of protocols is essential for diagnosing issues, detecting anomalies, and optimizing network performance.

Wireshark also allows you to export captured data for further analysis or archival purposes.

You can save captured packets in various formats, including the widely used PCAP format, which is compatible with many other network analysis tools.

Exported data can be shared with colleagues, imported into other analysis tools, or stored for future reference.

When configuring Wireshark for advanced analysis, it's essential to keep your analysis goals in mind.

Consider the specific network issues you're trying to address, the protocols involved, and the data you need to capture.

By tailoring your configuration, using display and capture filters effectively, leveraging profiles, and utilizing

Wireshark's numerous features, you can conduct in-depth network analysis efficiently and effectively.

Wireshark's flexibility, combined with your expertise, makes it a valuable tool for advanced network analysis and troubleshooting.

In summary, configuring Wireshark for advanced analysis is a crucial step in harnessing the power of this network protocol analyzer for troubleshooting, security assessment, and performance optimization.

Chapter 3: Passive Reconnaissance with Kismet

Passive reconnaissance techniques play a vital role in gathering information about a target or network without directly interacting with it.

This phase of the reconnaissance process focuses on collecting publicly available data from various sources to build an initial understanding of the target's infrastructure and potential vulnerabilities.

Passive reconnaissance is often the first step in a comprehensive security assessment or ethical hacking engagement.

One of the primary goals of passive reconnaissance is to gather as much information as possible about the target while avoiding any actions that could trigger alerts or raise suspicion.

This approach allows security professionals and ethical hackers to conduct a thorough assessment while minimizing the risk of detection.

Passive reconnaissance techniques leverage open-source intelligence (OSINT) to gather information from publicly accessible sources, such as websites, social media profiles, and domain registration records.

For example, searching for the target's domain name or organization name in search engines can yield valuable insights.

By reviewing search results, an attacker can discover publicly available documents, web pages, or mentions of the target, providing clues about its infrastructure and online presence.

Domain registration records are another valuable source of information during passive reconnaissance.

These records, often accessible through WHOIS databases, contain details about the domain's owner, registration date, and contact information.

Analyzing WHOIS data can help identify the organization behind a website, potential third-party service providers, and even email addresses associated with the domain.

In addition to WHOIS data, passive reconnaissance may involve querying public DNS records to discover subdomains associated with the target.

Tools like DNS enumeration scripts or online services can assist in identifying additional hostnames that might be part of the target's infrastructure.

Subdomain enumeration can reveal potentially overlooked entry points or weak links in the security chain.

Publicly available databases, such as the National Vulnerability Database (NVD), provide a wealth of information about known vulnerabilities in software, operating systems, and applications.

During passive reconnaissance, security professionals may search these databases to identify vulnerabilities associated with the target's technology stack.

This information can help prioritize later stages of the assessment, focusing on potential weaknesses that could be exploited.

Social media platforms are often treasure troves of information for passive reconnaissance.

Analyzing an organization's or individual's social media profiles can reveal employee names, job titles, and even details about their work responsibilities.

Attackers can piece together this information to craft convincing social engineering attacks or gain insights into an organization's internal structure.

LinkedIn, for example, is a valuable resource for gathering professional information about employees and their roles within an organization.

Passive reconnaissance may also involve scanning public forums, discussion boards, or mailing lists for discussions related to the target.

These online communities can provide valuable insights into the target's technology stack, challenges, and potential vulnerabilities.

By monitoring discussions, an attacker can gain knowledge about the tools and technologies in use, which may inform later stages of the assessment.

Email addresses are a valuable asset for passive reconnaissance, as they can serve as potential points of entry or attack vectors.

Publicly available email addresses associated with the target organization can be identified through website contact pages, social media profiles, or online publications.

Collecting these addresses enables an attacker to perform reconnaissance on email security measures and potentially craft spear-phishing or social engineering attacks.

Passive reconnaissance can also extend to the analysis of SSL/TLS certificates.

By examining certificate information, an attacker can gain insights into the target's infrastructure and web services.

Certificates often include details such as domain names, issue dates, and expiration dates, which can help map out the target's digital footprint.

While passive reconnaissance techniques focus on gathering publicly available information, it's crucial to approach this phase with a responsible and ethical mindset.

Respecting privacy, adhering to legal and ethical boundaries, and obtaining proper authorization are fundamental principles of ethical hacking and security assessments.

The information collected during passive reconnaissance serves as a foundation for subsequent phases of an assessment, such as active scanning and vulnerability analysis.

It allows security professionals and ethical hackers to develop a comprehensive understanding of the target's digital landscape, potential vulnerabilities, and areas of focus.

Ultimately, passive reconnaissance techniques are an essential component of a thorough security assessment, helping organizations identify and address weaknesses in their infrastructure before malicious actors can exploit them.

By leveraging publicly available data and adhering to ethical guidelines, security professionals can enhance their ability to protect networks and assets from potential threats.

Kismet is a powerful open-source wireless network detection, sniffing, and intrusion detection system that is widely used in the field of wireless security and ethical hacking.

It provides a robust set of features for both passive and active wireless reconnaissance, making it an invaluable tool for gathering valuable information about wireless networks and devices.

Kismet's primary purpose is to detect and analyze wireless networks, including Wi-Fi networks, Bluetooth devices, and other wireless protocols, within its range.

It operates in a passive mode, which means it does not actively transmit any data, making it difficult for network administrators to detect its presence.

One of Kismet's key capabilities is its ability to capture wireless data packets from nearby networks.

It can listen to network traffic, analyze packets, and extract useful information, such as SSIDs (Service Set Identifiers), MAC addresses, signal strengths, and encryption types.

By capturing this data, Kismet enables security professionals and ethical hackers to identify nearby wireless networks and gather essential information about their configurations.

Kismet provides support for various wireless interfaces and hardware, allowing users to choose the most suitable equipment for their specific needs.

This flexibility ensures that Kismet can be used with a wide range of wireless adapters, making it adaptable to different hardware environments.

Once Kismet is up and running, it continuously monitors the airwaves, identifying nearby wireless networks and devices.

It can also detect hidden networks that do not broadcast their SSIDs, providing insights into networks that may be attempting to remain discreet.

In addition to capturing basic network information, Kismet can conduct more advanced wireless reconnaissance tasks.

For example, it can track the movement of wireless devices as they connect and disconnect from various access points.

This tracking can be useful for identifying patterns of behavior or determining the physical locations of devices within the network's coverage area.

Kismet's logging and reporting capabilities are crucial for documenting the information gathered during wireless reconnaissance.

It can log data to various file formats, including PCAP (Packet Capture) files, which are compatible with tools like Wireshark for in-depth analysis.

Users can also configure Kismet to generate reports summarizing the discovered networks, devices, and other relevant details.

These reports are valuable for both understanding the wireless environment and presenting findings to stakeholders.

Kismet's support for plugins and extensions further extends its functionality.

Users can add custom plugins to enhance its capabilities, such as integrating with geolocation services to map the physical locations of wireless networks.

This feature can be particularly valuable for security assessments or site surveys.

Kismet also includes a web-based user interface that provides real-time visualization of detected wireless networks on a map.

This graphical representation allows users to quickly identify the spatial distribution of networks and devices, aiding in situational awareness.

Kismet can be configured to send alerts or notifications when specific events occur, such as the detection of rogue access points or unauthorized devices.

These alerts can help security professionals respond promptly to potential threats or security incidents.

When conducting ethical hacking or security assessments, Kismet's passive reconnaissance capabilities are essential for gathering information about the target's wireless infrastructure.

By understanding the wireless networks in use, their configurations, and the devices connected to them, ethical hackers can identify potential vulnerabilities and security weaknesses.

Kismet's stealthy operation ensures that it can collect valuable data without alerting network administrators or raising suspicions.

However, it's important to note that using Kismet for wireless reconnaissance should always be done within the boundaries of ethical and legal guidelines.

Unauthorized wireless network monitoring may be subject to legal restrictions, and obtaining proper authorization is a fundamental ethical principle.

In summary, Kismet is a versatile and powerful tool for gathering valuable information about wireless networks and devices.

Its passive reconnaissance capabilities, support for various wireless interfaces, logging and reporting features, and extensibility through plugins make it a valuable asset for security professionals and ethical hackers.

By using Kismet responsibly and within the bounds of ethical and legal considerations, individuals and organizations can enhance their understanding of wireless environments and improve their security posture.

Chapter 4: Active Reconnaissance with Kismet

Active reconnaissance methods are a crucial component of the information-gathering phase in ethical hacking and security assessments.

Unlike passive reconnaissance, which focuses on collecting publicly available data, active reconnaissance involves actively probing and interacting with the target network or system to gather information.

Active reconnaissance techniques are essential for identifying vulnerabilities, potential entry points, and security weaknesses within a network or infrastructure.

These methods typically involve sending requests, scanning for open ports, and probing network services to gain insights into the target's configuration and potential vulnerabilities.

One of the primary goals of active reconnaissance is to obtain a more comprehensive understanding of the target environment by directly interacting with it.

Active reconnaissance often starts with network scanning, where an ethical hacker uses various tools and techniques to discover hosts, services, and open ports within the target network.

By probing the target's network, an attacker can identify live hosts, their IP addresses, and the services running on them.

This information is critical for creating a network map and understanding the scope of the target environment.

One common active reconnaissance technique is the use of port scanning tools like Nmap, which send packets to target hosts to determine which ports are open and what services are running.

Port scanning helps identify potential entry points and services that may be susceptible to attacks.

Another active reconnaissance method involves banner grabbing, where an attacker connects to open ports on target hosts and collects information from the banners or responses provided by the services.

Banner grabbing can reveal the software versions, operating systems, and configurations of the services running on the target hosts.

This information is valuable for identifying potential vulnerabilities that are specific to certain software versions.

Ethical hackers also employ vulnerability scanning tools during active reconnaissance.

These tools automatically scan the target network for known vulnerabilities in services, operating systems, and applications.

Vulnerability scanners like Nessus and OpenVAS can help identify weaknesses that could be exploited by attackers.

Active reconnaissance may also involve network enumeration, which is the process of identifying active hosts, shared resources, and user accounts within the target environment.

Enumeration techniques can provide valuable insights into the network's structure, user privileges, and potential attack vectors.

Attackers often use DNS enumeration to discover subdomains and gather information about the target's domain name system.

By querying DNS servers, an attacker can find additional hostnames and IP addresses associated with the target organization.

Active reconnaissance is not limited to scanning and enumeration; it also includes techniques like service probing and fingerprinting.

Service probing involves interacting with network services to gather more information about their configurations and potential vulnerabilities.

Fingerprinting, on the other hand, aims to identify the specific software and versions used by network services, which helps attackers tailor their attacks.

Ethical hackers may employ brute-force attacks as part of their active reconnaissance efforts to crack passwords or gain unauthorized access to network resources.

These attacks involve attempting multiple username and password combinations until the correct credentials are found.

Brute-force attacks can be time-consuming but can reveal weak or easily guessable passwords within the target environment.

Active reconnaissance techniques also encompass traffic analysis, where an attacker captures and analyzes network traffic to gain insights into the target's communication patterns, protocols, and data flows.

By examining network traffic, an attacker can identify potential vulnerabilities or security weaknesses, such as unencrypted data transmissions.

While active reconnaissance methods are essential for ethical hacking and security assessments, they must be conducted responsibly and ethically.

Gaining proper authorization and adhering to legal and ethical boundaries are paramount when conducting active reconnaissance.

Unauthorized probing and scanning of networks can disrupt operations, violate privacy, and lead to legal consequences.

Ethical hackers should always obtain explicit permission from the target organization and ensure that their actions do not cause harm or disruptions.

In summary, active reconnaissance methods are a critical part of the ethical hacking process, enabling security professionals to gather essential information about target networks and systems.

These techniques, including network scanning, port scanning, vulnerability scanning, enumeration, and fingerprinting, provide insights into potential vulnerabilities and weaknesses that may be exploited by malicious actors.

However, conducting active reconnaissance requires a responsible and ethical approach, with a focus on obtaining proper authorization and respecting legal boundaries to ensure the security and privacy of target organizations.

Conducting targeted scans with Kismet is a strategic approach to wireless network reconnaissance, allowing ethical hackers and security professionals to focus on specific areas of interest within a wireless environment. While Kismet is known for its passive reconnaissance capabilities, it also offers features for actively scanning and analyzing wireless networks.
Targeted scans are particularly valuable when an ethical hacker wants to investigate specific wireless access points, devices, or areas of concern within the target environment.

Kismet's ability to perform targeted scans enables security professionals to gather detailed information about specific networks or devices that may be of interest during security assessments.
To conduct targeted scans with Kismet, users can leverage its active scanning features to gain insights into the networks and devices within a specific area.
This approach can be useful for identifying potential vulnerabilities, rogue access points, or unauthorized devices that require further examination.
One common use case for targeted scans with Kismet is the identification of rogue access points.
Rogue access points are unauthorized wireless access points that can pose a security risk to an organization by providing an entry point for attackers.

By actively scanning for wireless access points within a specific range, security professionals can identify any rogue access points that may be present within the target environment.

Kismet allows users to specify the frequency range and channels to scan, enabling them to focus on a specific area of interest.

This level of granularity ensures that the scan is tailored to the target's wireless infrastructure and objectives.

Targeted scans with Kismet can also be used to assess the security of specific networks or access points.

Security professionals can actively probe the target network to identify open ports, services, and potential vulnerabilities.

By scanning for open ports and services, ethical hackers can determine if there are any misconfigured or unprotected services that could be exploited by attackers.

Additionally, targeted scans can help identify weak encryption methods or default configurations that need to be addressed.

Kismet's active scanning capabilities extend to wireless devices as well.

Ethical hackers can conduct targeted scans to identify and analyze specific wireless devices within the network.

This includes smartphones, laptops, IoT devices, and other wireless endpoints.

By actively scanning and profiling these devices, security professionals can assess their security posture and identify any vulnerabilities or misconfigurations that may be present.

In situations where a security assessment is focused on a specific area or location, targeted scans with Kismet can provide detailed insights into the wireless environment within that area.

For example, if an organization wants to assess the security of its guest network in a conference room, targeted scans can be performed in that location to identify potential issues.

Kismet's scanning capabilities are not limited to Wi-Fi networks alone.

It can also scan and analyze other wireless protocols, such as Bluetooth and Zigbee, making it versatile for assessing a wide range of wireless technologies.

To conduct a targeted scan with Kismet, users can set up the desired scan parameters, including frequency bands, channels, and scan duration.

Once the scan is initiated, Kismet actively probes the specified area, collecting information about wireless networks, devices, and services.

The collected data is then logged and can be further analyzed to identify security issues or vulnerabilities.

However, it's essential to note that conducting targeted scans with Kismet, or any other scanning tool, should always be done within the boundaries of ethical and legal guidelines.

Obtaining proper authorization and ensuring compliance with relevant laws and regulations is crucial to conducting ethical and responsible security assessments.

In summary, conducting targeted scans with Kismet is a valuable approach for wireless network reconnaissance, allowing security professionals to focus on specific areas or objectives within a wireless environment.

By actively scanning for wireless access points, devices, and services, ethical hackers can identify potential vulnerabilities, rogue access points, and security issues that require further attention.

However, ethical and legal considerations must always be prioritized when conducting targeted scans to ensure responsible and ethical security assessments.

Chapter 5: Advanced Wi-Fi Packet Capture with Wireshark

Enhancing Wi-Fi packet capture is a critical aspect of wireless network analysis and security assessment, allowing professionals to gain deeper insights into network traffic and potential security threats.

Packet capture, also known as packet sniffing or network traffic analysis, involves intercepting and recording data packets as they traverse a wireless network.

It provides valuable information about the communication between devices, the types of traffic being transmitted, and potential anomalies or security issues.

To enhance Wi-Fi packet capture, it's essential to use specialized tools and techniques that can capture and analyze packets effectively.

One of the most widely used packet capture tools for Wi-Fi networks is Wireshark, a powerful and versatile network protocol analyzer.

Wireshark allows security professionals to capture, inspect, and dissect data packets in real-time, making it an invaluable tool for network analysis.

To enhance packet capture with Wireshark, users can follow best practices for configuring and utilizing the software effectively.

This includes selecting the appropriate wireless interface for capturing packets, setting capture filters to focus on specific traffic, and utilizing display filters to narrow down the packets of interest.

Enhancing packet capture with Wireshark also involves understanding the different wireless protocols and their associated headers.

Wi-Fi packets contain various layers, including the physical layer (PHY), data link layer (MAC), and network layer (IP), each with its own set of headers.

By understanding these headers and their significance, security professionals can extract valuable information from captured packets.

Furthermore, packet capture can be enhanced by utilizing advanced features within Wireshark, such as protocol analysis, flow tracking, and conversation reconstruction.

These features enable users to analyze network behavior, identify patterns, and detect potential anomalies or security incidents.

In addition to Wireshark, other specialized tools and hardware devices can enhance Wi-Fi packet capture.

Wireless network adapters that support monitor mode and packet injection are essential for capturing packets effectively.

These adapters allow professionals to sniff wireless traffic without being connected to a specific network and inject packets for various testing and analysis purposes.

To enhance packet capture capabilities further, professionals can employ external antennas and signal amplifiers to improve reception and capture distant or weak signals.

Enhancing Wi-Fi packet capture also involves optimizing the capture process for specific objectives, such as monitoring network performance, troubleshooting connectivity issues, or identifying security threats.

For performance monitoring, professionals may focus on capturing packets related to network throughput, latency, and application performance.

Troubleshooting connectivity issues may require capturing packets related to connection establishment, authentication, and error messages.

In the case of security assessments, enhancing packet capture involves looking for signs of malicious activity, unauthorized access, or suspicious traffic patterns.

To effectively enhance packet capture for security purposes, professionals can employ intrusion detection systems (IDS) or intrusion prevention systems (IPS) that analyze network traffic in real-time and generate alerts for potential threats.

Enhancing packet capture for security also includes capturing authentication handshakes, identifying potential rogue access points, and monitoring for unusual or unauthorized behavior.

Furthermore, professionals can employ packet capture techniques to identify security vulnerabilities, such as weak encryption methods or unpatched software.

To enhance packet capture for vulnerability assessment, tools like Nessus or OpenVAS can be used to scan captured packets for known vulnerabilities in network services and applications.

Packet capture can also be enhanced by leveraging cloud-based analysis platforms that provide real-time threat detection and analysis capabilities.

These platforms can process large volumes of captured packets and identify security incidents quickly, reducing the time required to respond to threats.

In summary, enhancing Wi-Fi packet capture is a crucial aspect of wireless network analysis and security assessment.

Professionals can achieve this by using specialized tools like Wireshark, optimizing capture settings, understanding wireless protocols, and utilizing advanced features.

Furthermore, employing specialized hardware, external antennas, and signal amplifiers can enhance packet capture capabilities.

Whether the goal is performance monitoring, troubleshooting, or security assessment, enhancing packet capture enables professionals to gain deeper insights into network traffic and potential security threats, ultimately improving the overall security and reliability of wireless networks.

Wireshark, as a powerful network protocol analyzer, offers a wide array of filters and display options that can significantly enhance the analysis of captured network traffic.

These filters and display options allow users to focus on specific packets, dissect protocols, and extract valuable information from the vast amount of data present in network captures.

One fundamental feature of Wireshark is its ability to apply display filters, which enable users to view only the packets that meet certain criteria.

Display filters can be based on various packet attributes, such as source and destination IP addresses, port numbers, protocol types, and more.

By specifying these filters, analysts can narrow down their view to packets relevant to their analysis, making it easier to identify specific network behaviors or issues.

Wireshark also provides a "display filter expression" field that allows users to input custom filter expressions using a powerful syntax, enabling complex and precise packet selection.

For example, a display filter expression like "ip.src == 192.168.1.1" would display only packets originating from the IP address 192.168.1.1.

Beyond display filters, Wireshark offers coloring rules that visually distinguish packets based on various criteria.

Coloring rules help users quickly identify packets of interest or potential issues, making it easier to spot anomalies in network traffic.

Users can customize these coloring rules to match their specific analysis needs.

Additionally, Wireshark provides a comprehensive set of protocol-specific filters that allow users to filter packets based on the specific protocol being used.

These filters make it convenient to focus on particular aspects of network communication, such as HTTP requests, DNS queries, or FTP transfers.

Wireshark's dissectors, which are responsible for parsing various network protocols, provide detailed information about each packet's structure and content.

This level of protocol analysis can be invaluable for understanding network behavior, diagnosing issues, and identifying security threats.

Wireshark's "Follow TCP Stream" and "Follow UDP Stream" options provide an even deeper level of insight. These features allow users to reconstruct and view the entire conversation between two endpoints, making it easier to comprehend the context of network traffic.

Wireshark's display options extend to packet details, where users can choose which fields and attributes they want to see.

This level of customization enables analysts to focus on the information most relevant to their analysis objectives.

Wireshark also offers the ability to export captured packets and analysis results to various file formats.

This functionality is valuable for sharing findings with colleagues, providing evidence for incident response, or archiving historical network captures.

Wireshark supports a range of output formats, including plain text, CSV, XML, and even pcapng, which is a common format for packet captures.

Furthermore, Wireshark's integrated statistics and analysis tools provide insights into network performance, trends, and anomalies.

These tools include packet summary statistics, protocol hierarchy statistics, and endpoint statistics, among others.

These statistics help users understand network behavior, identify patterns, and pinpoint areas that may require further investigation.

In addition to its graphical user interface (GUI), Wireshark offers a command-line version called "tshark," which provides similar filtering and analysis capabilities.

This command-line tool is especially useful for batch processing and scripting, making it a valuable asset for automating network analysis tasks.

Wireshark's flexibility and extensibility are further enhanced by its support for custom Lua scripts and dissectors.

This allows advanced users to create their own dissectors or add custom functionality to Wireshark to suit their specific needs.

Wireshark's "Expert Info" feature is yet another valuable tool that highlights potential issues and anomalies in captured packets.

These warnings and suggestions can help analysts quickly identify and address problems in the network.

In summary, Wireshark's extensive array of filters and display options, coupled with its advanced protocol analysis capabilities, make it a versatile and indispensable tool for network professionals, security analysts, and anyone tasked with understanding and troubleshooting network traffic.

By leveraging these features effectively, users can streamline their analysis, gain deeper insights into network behavior, and pinpoint issues that may require attention, ultimately improving the reliability and security of network communications.

Chapter 6: Wireless Traffic Analysis and Decryption

Decrypting encrypted wireless traffic is a complex process that involves unraveling the encryption applied to the data packets transmitted over a wireless network.

This process is crucial for security professionals, ethical hackers, and network administrators who need to inspect, analyze, or monitor network traffic that is protected by encryption.

Encryption is used to secure the confidentiality and integrity of data as it traverses a wireless network, making it unreadable to unauthorized parties.

However, in certain scenarios, decrypting this traffic is necessary to detect security vulnerabilities, identify malicious activities, or troubleshoot network issues.

To decrypt encrypted wireless traffic, one must possess the necessary cryptographic keys used to encrypt and decrypt the data.

In the context of Wi-Fi networks, the two most common encryption protocols are WEP (Wired Equivalent Privacy) and WPA/WPA2 (Wi-Fi Protected Access).

WEP encryption is relatively weak and can be decrypted using various methods, making it an easier target for decryption.

WPA/WPA2, on the other hand, is more robust and secure, but it can still be decrypted under specific conditions, such as weak passwords or flawed implementations.

To decrypt WEP-encrypted traffic, one typically needs access to the WEP key used by the network.

This key can be obtained through various means, such as exploiting vulnerabilities in the WEP protocol, capturing an authentication handshake, or using known attack methods like ARP (Address Resolution Protocol) replay attacks.

Once the WEP key is obtained, it can be used to decrypt the data packets captured from the network.

Decrypting WPA/WPA2-encrypted traffic is considerably more challenging due to the stronger security mechanisms in place.

To decrypt WPA/WPA2-encrypted traffic, one must obtain the Pre-Shared Key (PSK) used for authentication and encryption.

The PSK is typically derived from a passphrase or a complex password chosen by the network administrator or the user.

In some cases, an attacker may attempt to crack the PSK using brute-force or dictionary attacks, but this process can be time-consuming and resource-intensive.

Alternatively, if an attacker captures the WPA/WPA2 handshake between a client device and the access point, they can attempt to brute-force the PSK offline using specialized tools and large wordlists.

Decrypting WPA/WPA2 traffic can also be accomplished if the PSK is weak or easily guessable.

In such cases, attackers can quickly recover the key and use it to decrypt the intercepted data packets.

However, it is essential to emphasize that attempting to decrypt encrypted wireless traffic without proper authorization is unethical and, in many cases, illegal.

Ethical hackers and security professionals should only perform decryption for legitimate security assessments and with the explicit consent of the network owner.

In some situations, authorized individuals may have access to the encryption keys or credentials required for decryption.

For example, a network administrator may need to decrypt wireless traffic to troubleshoot network issues, monitor for malicious activities, or comply with regulatory requirements.

In such cases, the administrator can configure network monitoring tools and security appliances to decrypt traffic using the authorized keys or credentials.

These tools can provide real-time visibility into network traffic, allowing administrators to identify and respond to security incidents promptly.

Decrypting encrypted wireless traffic can also be essential for network forensics, where investigators need to reconstruct network communications to understand security breaches or incidents fully.

Forensic analysts can use specialized tools and techniques to decrypt captured traffic and analyze it for evidence of malicious activities or unauthorized access.

Additionally, decrypting encrypted wireless traffic is vital for intrusion detection systems (IDS) and intrusion prevention systems (IPS).

These security solutions monitor network traffic for suspicious or malicious patterns and may require access to decrypted traffic to accurately detect and respond to threats.

To ensure the secure decryption of wireless traffic, it is crucial to implement strong security practices and safeguard the encryption keys and credentials.

Keys should be regularly rotated, and strong, unique passwords should be used for encryption to minimize the risk of unauthorized decryption.

In summary, decrypting encrypted wireless traffic is a complex and sensitive task that requires access to encryption keys or credentials.

While it is crucial for security professionals, network administrators, and forensic analysts, it should only be conducted with proper authorization and ethical considerations.

Unauthorized decryption attempts are unethical and illegal, and they can have severe legal consequences.

By following best practices and obtaining proper consent, professionals can use decryption techniques to enhance network security, troubleshoot issues, and investigate security incidents effectively.

Analyzing network behavior and patterns is a fundamental aspect of network monitoring and security.

By closely examining how data flows within a network, professionals can gain valuable insights into its performance and potential security threats.

Network behavior analysis involves the systematic observation of traffic patterns, data transfers, and communication protocols within a network environment.

One of the primary goals of this analysis is to identify anomalies or deviations from established norms, which could indicate security breaches or operational issues.

Analyzing network behavior and patterns is a proactive approach to maintaining network health and security.

This process enables organizations to detect and address issues before they escalate into significant problems.

Anomalies in network behavior can manifest in various ways, such as unusual spikes in data traffic, unauthorized access attempts, unexpected protocol usage, or deviations from typical usage patterns.

To effectively analyze network behavior, professionals employ a range of tools and techniques.

Network monitoring solutions, such as intrusion detection systems (IDS) and network traffic analyzers, continuously collect data from various points within the network.

This data includes packet captures, log files, and metadata that provide comprehensive information about network activity.

By processing and analyzing this data, professionals can create baseline models of normal network behavior.

These models serve as references for identifying deviations or unusual patterns that may indicate security incidents or performance problems.

One common approach to analyzing network behavior is anomaly detection.

This method involves the use of machine learning algorithms and statistical models to automatically identify deviations from established baselines.

For example, an IDS can employ anomaly detection to flag network traffic that exhibits unexpected or suspicious behavior.

Professionals can configure alerting mechanisms to notify them when anomalies are detected, allowing for swift investigation and response.

In addition to identifying security threats, analyzing network behavior can help optimize network performance.

By studying traffic patterns, organizations can identify bottlenecks, network congestion, or resource utilization issues.

This information enables network administrators to make informed decisions regarding capacity planning, resource allocation, and network design improvements.

Another critical aspect of network behavior analysis is the identification of patterns related to specific applications or services.

This information is valuable for optimizing network performance and ensuring the efficient delivery of critical services.

For example, by analyzing the behavior of a video conferencing application, administrators can allocate sufficient bandwidth to ensure a smooth user experience.

Analyzing network behavior also plays a crucial role in identifying and mitigating distributed denial of service (DDoS) attacks.

DDoS attacks involve overwhelming a target network or service with an excessive volume of traffic.

By monitoring network behavior, professionals can detect sudden increases in traffic that may indicate a DDoS attack in progress.

Prompt detection allows organizations to implement countermeasures, such as traffic filtering or rate limiting, to mitigate the impact of the attack.

Furthermore, analyzing network behavior is essential for compliance and regulatory purposes.

Many industries and organizations are subject to data protection laws and regulations that require monitoring and auditing network activities.

Network behavior analysis tools can provide detailed reports and logs to demonstrate compliance with these requirements.

Network administrators and security professionals also rely on behavioral analysis to identify unauthorized or malicious activities within a network.

For example, detecting repeated failed login attempts or unusual data exfiltration patterns can help uncover security breaches.

By closely examining network behavior, organizations can uncover signs of insider threats or compromised systems.

In summary, analyzing network behavior and patterns is a multifaceted process with significant benefits for network performance and security.

By continuously monitoring and assessing traffic, professionals can identify anomalies, optimize network resources, detect security threats, and ensure compliance with regulations.

This proactive approach empowers organizations to maintain a robust and secure network environment while providing a seamless experience for users and customers.

Chapter 7: Analyzing Mobile Device Traffic

Capturing mobile device traffic is a critical aspect of network monitoring and cybersecurity, given the increasing prevalence of mobile devices in our daily lives.

Mobile devices, such as smartphones and tablets, have become ubiquitous tools for communication, productivity, and entertainment, making them valuable targets for both legitimate and malicious purposes.

To capture mobile device traffic effectively, it is essential to understand the unique challenges and considerations associated with these devices.

Mobile devices connect to wireless networks, cellular networks, and the internet, often simultaneously, creating complex traffic patterns that must be analyzed comprehensively.

The first step in capturing mobile device traffic is to select the appropriate tools and methodologies.

There are various methods to capture mobile device traffic, each with its advantages and limitations.

One common approach is to use network monitoring tools and solutions that are compatible with mobile devices.

These tools can intercept and analyze network traffic as it flows through the device, providing valuable insights into communication patterns, application usage, and potential security threats.

For Android devices, applications like Wireshark for Android and tPacketCapture allow users to capture and analyze network traffic on their devices.

On iOS devices, Packet Capture and Charles Proxy offer similar capabilities.

It is essential to ensure that these tools are used responsibly and in compliance with legal and ethical guidelines.

Another approach to capturing mobile device traffic is through the use of mobile device management (MDM) solutions.

MDM solutions are often employed by organizations to manage and secure mobile devices used by their employees.

These solutions can capture traffic data and provide insights into device usage, including application usage, data transfer volumes, and potential security risks.

While MDM solutions are primarily designed for device management and security, they can serve as valuable sources of traffic data for analysis.

Mobile carriers also play a crucial role in capturing mobile device traffic, as they are responsible for routing data between mobile devices and the internet.

Mobile carriers have the capability to capture traffic at various points within their networks, allowing them to monitor and analyze traffic patterns for both operational and security purposes.

For example, carriers may detect and mitigate DDoS attacks or identify unusual data usage that could indicate fraudulent activities.

Capturing mobile device traffic for security analysis involves monitoring communication between mobile devices and external servers or services.

This communication can include web browsing, email, messaging applications, and more.

By capturing and analyzing this traffic, organizations can identify potential security threats, such as malware infections, phishing attacks, or data breaches.

For example, if a mobile device sends sensitive information over an unsecured connection, such as login credentials or financial data, it could be intercepted and exploited by malicious actors.

Capturing mobile device traffic can help detect such risky behaviors and mitigate security risks.

Additionally, capturing mobile device traffic is valuable for understanding the privacy implications of mobile applications.

Many mobile applications collect and transmit user data to external servers for various purposes, such as advertising, analytics, and user profiling.

Analyzing the traffic generated by these applications can reveal the extent of data collection and potential privacy violations.

This information is crucial for both users and regulatory authorities concerned with data privacy.

Capturing mobile device traffic also plays a role in network troubleshooting and optimization.

Network administrators can use traffic data to identify performance bottlenecks, network congestion, or quality of service (QoS) issues affecting mobile users.

By analyzing traffic patterns, administrators can make informed decisions about network optimization and capacity planning to ensure a seamless user experience.

Furthermore, capturing mobile device traffic can aid in forensic investigations.

In the event of a security incident or data breach involving a mobile device, forensic analysts can examine traffic data to reconstruct the sequence of events and determine the scope of the breach.

This information is invaluable for legal proceedings and incident response.

In summary, capturing mobile device traffic is a multifaceted process with significant implications for network security, privacy, optimization, and forensic analysis.

Professionals must carefully choose the appropriate tools and methods while adhering to legal and ethical guidelines.

By capturing and analyzing mobile device traffic, organizations can enhance their cybersecurity posture, protect user privacy, and optimize network performance.

Analyzing mobile app communication is a critical aspect of understanding the behavior and security of mobile applications.

Mobile apps are pervasive in today's digital landscape, offering a wide range of functionalities, from social networking to online banking.

To ensure the safety and privacy of users, it is essential to scrutinize how these apps communicate with external servers and services.

Mobile app communication encompasses the data exchanges that occur between a mobile app and remote servers or application programming interfaces (APIs).

This communication can involve various types of data, including user inputs, authentication credentials, location information, and more.

Analyzing this communication can reveal insights into an app's functionality, data handling practices, and potential security vulnerabilities.

One of the primary goals of analyzing mobile app communication is to identify and assess potential security risks.

Mobile apps often transmit sensitive information, such as login credentials or personal data, over the network.

This data must be adequately protected to prevent interception or unauthorized access.

By inspecting app communication, security professionals can detect improper data handling, unencrypted transmission, or inadequate authentication mechanisms that may put user data at risk.

For example, if an app sends login credentials in plaintext over an unsecured connection, it could expose users to credential theft.

Analyzing mobile app communication can also help identify potential privacy violations.

Many mobile apps collect and transmit user data to external servers for various purposes, including advertising, analytics, and user profiling.

Understanding how apps handle user data is essential for assessing privacy risks and ensuring compliance with data protection regulations.

For instance, if an app shares location data with third-party advertising networks without user consent, it may violate privacy regulations.

Analyzing app communication can reveal such practices.

To analyze mobile app communication, security professionals use a variety of tools and techniques.

One common approach is to intercept and inspect network traffic between the mobile device and remote servers.

Tools like Burp Suite, Charles Proxy, or Wireshark can capture and analyze network packets, providing a detailed view of the data exchanged during app communication.

By examining these packets, analysts can identify potential vulnerabilities or privacy concerns.

Another technique involves decompiling and reverse engineering the app's source code.

This allows analysts to examine how the app interacts with APIs and servers and to inspect the logic responsible for data handling.

Additionally, dynamic analysis of app behavior on a test device or emulator can provide insights into communication patterns and potential security flaws.

For instance, analysts can use tools like Frida or Mobile Security Framework (MobSF) to perform runtime analysis of app behavior.

Analyzing mobile app communication is crucial for both security researchers and developers.

Security researchers can uncover vulnerabilities and privacy issues that may require remediation.

Developers can use communication analysis to ensure that their apps adhere to best practices in data security and privacy.

Furthermore, mobile app communication analysis plays a vital role in compliance and regulatory requirements.

In many regions, data protection laws require organizations to inform users about data collection and obtain their consent.

Analyzing app communication helps organizations demonstrate compliance with these regulations by identifying data flows and data-sharing practices.

In summary, analyzing mobile app communication is a critical component of mobile app security and privacy.

It enables the detection of security vulnerabilities, privacy violations, and compliance issues.

By scrutinizing how mobile apps handle data and communicate with external servers, organizations can protect user data, maintain user trust, and ensure the security of their mobile applications.

Chapter 8: Detecting and Responding to Wireless Attacks

Identifying common wireless attacks is essential for securing wireless networks against malicious threats and vulnerabilities.

Wireless networks are susceptible to a variety of attacks due to their inherent nature of broadcasting signals over the airwaves.

By understanding these common wireless attacks, network administrators and security professionals can take proactive measures to protect their networks and data.

One of the most prevalent wireless attacks is the "Man-in-the-Middle" (MitM) attack.

In a MitM attack, an attacker intercepts and possibly alters the communication between two parties without their knowledge.

This attack is particularly dangerous in wireless networks, as it can be carried out in close proximity to the target network, such as in a coffee shop or airport.

To counter MitM attacks, network administrators should implement strong encryption protocols, such as WPA3, and use secure VPNs for remote connections.

Another common wireless attack is the "Evil Twin" or rogue access point attack.

In this attack, an attacker sets up a fake wireless access point with a name similar to a legitimate one, tricking users into connecting to it.

Once connected, the attacker can intercept and manipulate the traffic.

Detecting and mitigating rogue access points can be challenging, but regular network monitoring and the use of intrusion detection systems can help identify them.

"Packet Sniffing" is another common wireless attack where an attacker captures and analyzes data packets transmitted over the network.

This can lead to the exposure of sensitive information, including usernames and passwords.

To prevent packet sniffing, administrators should use encryption protocols like WPA3 and regularly monitor network traffic for suspicious activities.

"Denial of Service" (DoS) attacks are also a threat to wireless networks.

In a DoS attack, an attacker floods the network with traffic, rendering it inaccessible to legitimate users.

This can disrupt network operations and lead to downtime.

To defend against DoS attacks, administrators should implement intrusion prevention systems (IPS) and maintain up-to-date firmware and security patches.

"Deauthentication" attacks are another form of wireless attack where an attacker sends deauthentication packets to disconnect users from the network.

This can be used for malicious purposes or to create opportunities for other attacks.

To mitigate deauthentication attacks, administrators can use intrusion detection systems and strong network authentication methods.

"Password Cracking" attacks target weak or default passwords used for wireless network access.

Attackers use tools like Aircrack-ng to crack WEP or WPA/WPA2 keys.

To defend against password cracking attacks, administrators should enforce strong password policies and regularly update passwords.

"War Driving" is a wireless attack where an attacker drives around searching for vulnerable wireless networks.

Once identified, the attacker can attempt to infiltrate these networks.

To prevent war driving attacks, network administrators should disable broadcasting of SSIDs and use strong encryption.

"Bluetooth Attacks" exploit vulnerabilities in Bluetooth connections, potentially compromising devices and data.

Security measures like disabling unnecessary Bluetooth services and keeping device firmware updated can help mitigate these attacks.

"Wi-Fi Phishing" attacks trick users into connecting to malicious Wi-Fi networks that appear legitimate.

These attacks can lead to data theft and compromise user privacy.

To protect against Wi-Fi phishing, users should be cautious when connecting to unfamiliar networks and verify network credentials.

"MAC Spoofing" is an attack where an attacker changes their device's MAC address to impersonate another device on the network.

This can be used to gain unauthorized access.

Network administrators should implement MAC address filtering and monitoring to detect and prevent MAC spoofing.

"DNS Spoofing" attacks manipulate the Domain Name System (DNS) to redirect users to malicious websites.

Network administrators should use DNSSEC to authenticate DNS responses and protect against these attacks.

In summary, identifying and understanding common wireless attacks is essential for securing wireless networks.

By implementing appropriate security measures and regularly monitoring network traffic, organizations can defend against these threats and maintain the integrity and confidentiality of their data.

Top of Form

Immediate and proactive responses to attacks are crucial to minimizing damage and protecting network assets.

When a security breach or cyberattack is detected, it is essential to act swiftly and decisively to mitigate its impact.

The first step in responding to an attack is to identify the nature and scope of the incident.

Is it a malware infection, a data breach, a DDoS attack, or some other type of security incident?

Understanding the specifics of the attack is essential for formulating an effective response plan.

In some cases, the attack may still be ongoing when detected, requiring immediate action to halt the attacker's activities.

For example, in the case of a DDoS attack, network administrators may need to implement traffic filtering or rerouting to mitigate the impact on network resources.

In the case of a malware infection, isolating affected systems from the network may be necessary to prevent the spread of the malware to other devices.

Once the immediate threat has been contained, it is essential to gather evidence and investigate the incident thoroughly.

This involves analyzing log files, network traffic, and system artifacts to determine how the attack occurred and what vulnerabilities were exploited.

Forensic analysis is crucial for understanding the attacker's tactics, techniques, and objectives.

Based on the findings of the investigation, organizations can develop a comprehensive incident response plan.

This plan outlines the steps to be taken to remediate the attack, recover from any damage, and prevent future incidents.

The incident response plan should also specify the roles and responsibilities of team members involved in the response effort.

In some cases, organizations may need to involve law enforcement or cybersecurity experts to assist with the investigation and response.

In addition to addressing the technical aspects of an attack, organizations must also consider the legal and regulatory implications.

Data breaches, for example, may trigger legal requirements to notify affected individuals and regulatory authorities.

Failure to comply with these requirements can result in significant legal and financial penalties.

Therefore, it is essential to have a legal and compliance team involved in the incident response process.

Communication is a critical aspect of incident response.

Organizations must have a clear communication plan in place to notify internal stakeholders, such as employees and management, as well as external parties, including customers, partners, and the media.

Timely and accurate communication can help manage the reputation damage that often accompanies a security incident.

It is important to be transparent about the incident without disclosing sensitive information that could further compromise security.

Remediation efforts should focus on patching vulnerabilities, removing malware, and restoring affected systems to normal operation.

This may involve reinstalling software, restoring backups, or rebuilding compromised servers.

The goal is to eliminate the root cause of the attack and prevent it from happening again.

In some cases, organizations may need to implement additional security measures, such as enhanced monitoring, access controls, or network segmentation, to strengthen their defenses against future attacks.

Once the incident has been resolved, it is essential to conduct a post-incident review to assess the effectiveness of the response and identify areas for improvement.

This review should include an evaluation of the incident response plan, communication processes, and technical controls.

Feedback from team members involved in the response effort should be collected and used to refine the incident response procedures.

It is also important to update security policies and procedures based on lessons learned from the incident.

In summary, immediate and proactive responses to attacks are critical for minimizing the impact of security incidents and protecting organizational assets.

A well-defined incident response plan, effective communication, thorough investigation, and remediation efforts are all essential components of a successful response.

Organizations must also consider the legal and regulatory aspects of an incident and conduct post-incident reviews to continuously improve their security posture.

Chapter 9: Wireless Network Troubleshooting with Wireshark

Troubleshooting common wireless issues is an essential skill for anyone responsible for maintaining a wireless network.

Wireless networks can encounter various problems that can disrupt connectivity and impact user experience.

Understanding how to diagnose and resolve these issues is crucial for ensuring a reliable and stable wireless network.

One of the most common wireless issues is a slow or unstable connection.

Users may experience sluggish internet speeds or frequent disconnections, which can be frustrating.

This problem can occur for various reasons, including interference from neighboring networks, outdated firmware, or hardware limitations.

To troubleshoot slow or unstable connections, start by checking the signal strength and quality of the wireless network.

Use tools like Wi-Fi analyzers or wireless site survey tools to identify sources of interference and select the optimal Wi-Fi channel.

Updating router firmware and drivers for client devices can also help improve performance.

Another common issue is poor coverage, where certain areas of a building or space have weak or no wireless signal.

This can be caused by the positioning of access points, physical obstacles, or the distance from the router.

To address poor coverage, consider adding additional access points strategically placed to fill coverage gaps.

Adjusting the transmit power and antenna orientation of access points can also help extend coverage.

Authentication and connection problems are also frequent wireless issues.

Users may encounter difficulties connecting to the network or experience repeated authentication failures.

These problems can be related to incorrect passwords, expired authentication certificates, or mismatched security settings.

Troubleshoot authentication and connection problems by verifying the network credentials, ensuring that the security settings match those on the client devices, and renewing or updating authentication certificates.

Intermittent connectivity issues, where the connection drops sporadically, can be challenging to diagnose.

These issues can result from a variety of factors, such as interference, hardware malfunctions, or overheating devices.

To troubleshoot intermittent connectivity problems, check for overheating routers or access points and ensure they have adequate ventilation.

Inspect cables and connectors for damage, and consider replacing any faulty hardware.

Interference from other wireless devices and appliances can also disrupt Wi-Fi signals.

Microwaves, cordless phones, and neighboring Wi-Fi networks can all contribute to interference.

To address interference issues, identify the sources of interference and minimize their impact.

Choose Wi-Fi channels with less interference, and consider using 5 GHz Wi-Fi bands, which are often less crowded than the 2.4 GHz band.

Security concerns are another category of wireless issues. Unauthorized access, weak encryption, or misconfigured security settings can expose the network to security risks.

To troubleshoot security-related issues, review and update security protocols and access controls.

Implement strong encryption methods, such as WPA3, and regularly change Wi-Fi passwords.

Security auditing tools can help identify vulnerabilities and potential threats.

Guest network issues, such as slow performance or connectivity problems for guest users, can also arise.

Guest networks are typically isolated from the main network, and issues may occur if the configuration is not correctly set up.

To troubleshoot guest network issues, review the guest network settings and ensure they are configured correctly.

Monitor bandwidth usage to prevent guests from consuming excessive resources.

Finally, firmware and software updates are crucial for resolving many wireless issues.

Router manufacturers often release firmware updates to address security vulnerabilities and improve performance.

Keeping routers, access points, and client devices up to date with the latest firmware and software patches can help prevent and resolve various problems.

In summary, troubleshooting common wireless issues is essential for maintaining a reliable and secure wireless network.

By addressing slow or unstable connections, poor coverage, authentication and connection problems, intermittent connectivity issues, interference, security concerns, guest network issues, and keeping firmware and software updated, network administrators can ensure that their wireless networks operate smoothly and provide a seamless user experience.

Using Wireshark for effective troubleshooting is a valuable skill for network administrators and IT professionals.
Wireshark is a powerful network protocol analyzer that allows users to capture, inspect, and analyze network traffic in real-time.
It provides detailed insights into network communication, helping identify and resolve various network issues.
Whether you're troubleshooting performance problems, diagnosing connectivity issues, or investigating security incidents, Wireshark is an indispensable tool.
One of the primary use cases for Wireshark is troubleshooting network performance problems.
Slow application response times, high latency, and packet loss can all impact user experience.
Wireshark enables you to capture network traffic and analyze it to pinpoint performance bottlenecks.
You can identify network congestion, inefficient protocols, or misconfigured devices that may be causing performance issues.
Wireshark also allows you to monitor bandwidth utilization, helping you ensure that network resources are used efficiently.
Another common troubleshooting scenario is diagnosing connectivity issues.

When users report problems accessing network resources or websites, it's essential to determine whether the issue is related to the network or the specific application.

Wireshark can capture packets during the connection attempt, helping you identify any errors or anomalies in the communication.

By examining the handshake process and the exchange of data packets, you can identify issues such as failed DNS resolution, incorrect IP configurations, or firewall restrictions.

Security incidents are a significant concern for organizations, and Wireshark can play a crucial role in investigating them.

Suspicious network behavior, unexpected traffic patterns, or unauthorized access attempts may indicate a security breach.

Wireshark can help you capture and analyze network traffic to uncover signs of malicious activity.

You can look for unusual network connections, traffic to known malicious domains, or attempts to exploit vulnerabilities.

Wireshark also allows you to examine payload data, which may contain clues about the nature of the attack or the compromised systems.

When dealing with security incidents, it's essential to act swiftly to contain the threat and mitigate any potential damage.

Intrusion detection systems (IDS) and intrusion prevention systems (IPS) can benefit from Wireshark's capabilities as well.

Wireshark can be used to analyze alerts generated by these systems, providing additional context and helping administrators make informed decisions about whether the alerts represent real threats.

Furthermore, Wireshark can assist in fine-tuning IDS/IPS rules and policies by allowing administrators to review captured packets and adjust detection criteria.

Wireshark's ability to analyze encrypted traffic is a valuable feature for troubleshooting and security purposes.

While encrypted traffic provides privacy and security, it can pose challenges when diagnosing issues.

Wireshark can decrypt encrypted traffic if you have access to the encryption keys, allowing you to inspect the content of encrypted packets.

This capability is particularly useful for identifying application-specific issues within encrypted connections.

Wireshark supports various encryption protocols, including SSL/TLS and SSH.

When using Wireshark for troubleshooting, it's essential to capture traffic at the right location in the network.

Placing the capture point too close to the source of the problem may result in incomplete data.

On the other hand, capturing traffic too far from the source may include irrelevant data, making analysis more challenging.

Understanding the network topology and the location of potential issues is crucial for effective troubleshooting with Wireshark.

Wireshark's packet filtering and display filtering capabilities allow you to focus on the specific packets of interest.

You can use capture filters to specify which packets to capture based on criteria such as source or destination IP address, port numbers, or protocols.

Display filters, on the other hand, allow you to filter and display only the relevant packets from the captured data.

By using filters judiciously, you can reduce the volume of captured data, making it easier to identify and analyze the packets relevant to your troubleshooting task.

When using Wireshark for troubleshooting, it's important to maintain proper documentation.

Document the troubleshooting process, including the problem description, steps taken, and findings.

Having a clear record of the troubleshooting process can be valuable for future reference and knowledge sharing.

Additionally, consider saving Wireshark capture files for later analysis or sharing with colleagues or vendors.

Wireshark supports multiple file formats, making it easy to store and exchange capture data.

Lastly, keep Wireshark and any relevant plugins or dissectors up to date.

The Wireshark community continuously releases updates to improve functionality, fix bugs, and address security vulnerabilities.

Regularly updating your Wireshark installation ensures that you have access to the latest features and enhancements.

In summary, using Wireshark for effective troubleshooting is an essential skill for network professionals.

Wireshark's capabilities for capturing, analyzing, and diagnosing network issues make it a valuable tool in various scenarios, from performance optimization to security incident response.

By mastering the use of Wireshark filters, understanding network topology, documenting the troubleshooting process, and staying up to date, you can leverage Wireshark's power to resolve network challenges efficiently and effectively.

Top of Form

Chapter 10: Case Studies in Advanced Wireless Network Analysis

Real-world case studies in wireless analysis provide valuable insights into the practical application of wireless network analysis techniques and tools.

These case studies showcase how professionals leverage wireless analysis to address specific challenges and improve network performance.
By examining real-world scenarios, readers can gain a deeper understanding of the complexities and nuances of wireless networks.

One common real-world use case for wireless analysis is optimizing Wi-Fi performance in a crowded environment.
Imagine a busy office building with multiple floors and numerous employees using Wi-Fi for their day-to-day tasks.
In such a scenario, wireless network congestion can lead to slow internet speeds and frustrated users.
By conducting a comprehensive wireless analysis, network administrators can identify the root causes of congestion.
They may discover that certain access points are overloaded with clients, while others are underutilized.
Through careful analysis, administrators can adjust access point configurations, allocate channels more efficiently, and balance client loads to improve overall network performance.
Another real-world case involves troubleshooting intermittent connectivity issues in a large warehouse.

In this scenario, warehouse employees rely on wireless handheld devices to manage inventory and process orders.

However, some devices experience sporadic disconnections, causing delays and operational disruptions.

A wireless analysis can help identify the areas within the warehouse where signal strength is weak or where interference is occurring.

By strategically placing additional access points and optimizing antenna configurations, administrators can mitigate connectivity issues and ensure uninterrupted operations.

Security is a paramount concern in wireless networks, and real-world case studies often revolve around detecting and responding to security threats.

Consider a corporate campus with a guest Wi-Fi network used by visitors and contractors.

The IT team receives reports of suspicious activity on the guest network, such as unauthorized access attempts and unusual traffic patterns.

In response, they employ wireless analysis tools to monitor network traffic and identify potential security breaches.

Through packet inspection and anomaly detection, they uncover a rogue access point set up by an unauthorized user attempting to intercept sensitive data.

By promptly isolating the rogue access point and strengthening security measures, the IT team safeguards the network from potential threats.

Real-world case studies also demonstrate the importance of continuous monitoring and proactive maintenance.

In a hospitality setting, where guest satisfaction is paramount, a hotel's Wi-Fi network plays a crucial role.

Guests expect seamless connectivity for work and leisure, and any network downtime can lead to dissatisfaction.

To ensure uninterrupted service, hotel IT staff conduct regular wireless analysis to monitor network performance and anticipate potential issues.

By identifying trends, such as increased guest usage during peak hours, they can allocate resources accordingly and implement load-balancing strategies to maintain high-quality Wi-Fi service.

Moreover, wireless analysis can be instrumental in troubleshooting and optimizing wireless networks for outdoor environments.

For instance, a public park offers free Wi-Fi to visitors, but complaints arise about slow and unreliable connectivity.

To address this, network administrators employ wireless analysis to assess the coverage area and signal strength of outdoor access points.

They also investigate potential sources of interference, such as nearby construction equipment or other electronic devices.

By making adjustments to access point locations and signal propagation, they enhance the park's Wi-Fi experience, making it more enjoyable for visitors.

Furthermore, real-world case studies illustrate the significance of collaboration among IT professionals and vendors.

In a corporate campus undergoing a network upgrade, administrators face challenges related to compatibility and performance.

By working closely with wireless analysis experts from their equipment vendor, they conduct thorough testing and analysis.

This collaboration helps identify and resolve compatibility issues, fine-tune configurations, and optimize the network's overall performance.

Such partnerships enable organizations to maximize the benefits of their wireless solutions.

These real-world case studies underscore the versatility of wireless analysis in various industries and environments.

Whether optimizing Wi-Fi performance, troubleshooting connectivity issues, enhancing security, or fine-tuning outdoor networks, wireless analysis plays a vital role in maintaining efficient and reliable wireless communication.

By learning from these practical examples, network professionals can apply similar strategies and techniques to address their unique challenges and achieve better wireless outcomes.

Applying lessons from case studies to your work is a crucial aspect of professional development in the field of wireless network analysis. These real-world examples serve as valuable learning experiences, offering insights and practical strategies that can be adapted to various scenarios.

When studying case studies, it's essential to identify the key takeaways and principles that can be applied to your own work. Each case study presents a unique set of challenges and solutions, but underlying principles often remain consistent.

One fundamental lesson from case studies is the importance of thorough analysis before implementing changes or solutions. Before making any adjustments to your wireless network, conduct a comprehensive analysis to understand the current state, identify pain points, and set clear objectives.

Consider a case study where an organization successfully addressed network congestion by redistributing clients among access points. The lesson here is that analyzing client load distribution and optimizing access point configurations can lead to improved network performance.

Another valuable lesson is the significance of proactive monitoring and maintenance. In case studies involving network downtime or performance issues, proactive measures, such as regular monitoring and preventive maintenance, were instrumental in preventing future problems.

For instance, if a case study highlights how a hotel's Wi-Fi network maintained high guest satisfaction through continuous monitoring and load balancing, you can apply similar practices to ensure consistent network performance in your own hospitality environment.

Security-related case studies provide insights into identifying and mitigating security threats. Lessons here emphasize the importance of monitoring network traffic, using intrusion detection systems, and staying vigilant against rogue access points and unauthorized access attempts.

Incorporating these security practices into your own network can help safeguard against potential threats and data breaches.

Case studies often showcase the value of collaboration and partnerships with vendors and experts. When faced with complex challenges or network upgrades, working closely with wireless analysis experts from your equipment vendor can lead to effective solutions and optimizations.

Furthermore, adaptability is a recurring theme in case studies. The ability to adjust configurations, access point locations, and antenna settings based on changing network demands is essential for maintaining optimal performance.

In case studies involving outdoor Wi-Fi deployments, the adaptability to address environmental factors and interference sources can be particularly beneficial.

Implementing lessons from case studies requires a structured approach. Start by defining clear objectives for your own network project or issue. What specific goals do you aim to achieve, and what challenges need to be overcome?

Next, conduct a thorough analysis of your network's current state. Collect data, perform assessments, and identify areas that require improvement or optimization. This initial analysis is crucial for informed decision-making.

Once you've gained a deep understanding of your network's challenges and opportunities, you can begin implementing changes or solutions. It's essential to prioritize actions based on their potential impact and feasibility.

Remember that not all lessons from case studies will directly apply to your situation. Adaptation and customization are key. Tailor the strategies and techniques to fit your network's unique requirements and constraints.
Continuous monitoring and evaluation are also vital aspects of applying lessons from case studies. After implementing changes, regularly assess the results and adjust your approach as needed. Monitoring helps you identify any new issues or opportunities for further improvement.

Furthermore, consider seeking input and feedback from your team or colleagues. Collaboration and collective insights can enhance the effectiveness of your network optimization efforts.
In summary, case studies provide valuable insights, best practices, and real-world examples that can significantly benefit your work in wireless network analysis. By identifying key lessons and applying them thoughtfully to your own projects, you can enhance network performance, security, and overall efficiency.
Remember that successful application of case study lessons requires a structured approach, adaptability, and ongoing monitoring. Embrace the opportunity to learn from others' experiences and continuously improve your wireless network management skills.

Conclusion

In the pages of "Wireless Exploits and Countermeasures: Kali Linux NetHunter, Aircrack-ng, Kismet, and Wireshark," readers have embarked on a comprehensive journey through the dynamic world of wireless network security and exploitation. This book bundle, consisting of four distinct volumes, has strived to provide a comprehensive understanding of wireless networks, from the fundamental concepts to advanced techniques and strategies.

In "Book 1 - Wireless Exploits and Countermeasures: A Beginner's Guide," we laid the foundation for readers new to the field, offering them a gentle introduction to wireless networks, their vulnerabilities, and the essential tools for securing them. With the fundamental knowledge gained from this volume, beginners can confidently move forward in their exploration of wireless security.

"Book 2 - Mastering Kali Linux NetHunter for Wireless Security" delved into the world of Kali Linux NetHunter, an advanced platform for wireless security assessments. Readers learned how to set up their NetHunter environment, perform advanced Wi-Fi scanning and reconnaissance, and execute a range of wireless exploits. This volume provided the expertise needed to become proficient in leveraging NetHunter for mobile security assessments.

"Book 3 - Aircrack-ng Techniques: Cracking WEP/WPA/WPA2 Keys" took readers on a deep dive into the intricacies of Aircrack-ng, a powerful suite of tools for cracking Wi-Fi encryption. From cracking WEP keys to tackling the more robust WPA and WPA2 protocols, this book equipped readers with the knowledge and techniques needed to identify vulnerabilities in wireless networks and strengthen their security.

"Book 4 - Kismet and Wireshark: Advanced Wireless Network Analysis" brought readers into the realm of advanced network analysis with Kismet and Wireshark. This volume explored passive and active reconnaissance, wireless packet capture, traffic analysis, and the detection and response to wireless attacks. Readers emerged from this book with a profound understanding of how to conduct in-depth wireless network assessments and troubleshoot complex issues.

Collectively, these four books have sought to empower readers with a holistic perspective on wireless network security. From novice to expert, each volume catered to a specific skill level, ensuring that readers could progress at their own pace. Throughout this journey, we have emphasized the significance of ethical hacking practices, responsible disclosure, and continuous learning.

As we conclude this book bundle, it is our hope that readers have not only gained valuable knowledge but also cultivated a mindset of ethical and responsible hacking. Wireless networks are an integral part of our interconnected world, and their security is paramount. By understanding both the exploits and countermeasures, readers are better equipped to protect their networks, devices, and data.

In an ever-evolving landscape of technology and security threats, the pursuit of knowledge is a lifelong endeavor. We encourage readers to continue exploring, experimenting, and staying updated in the dynamic field of wireless network security. With the insights and skills acquired from these volumes, you are well-prepared to face the challenges and opportunities that lie ahead in the world of wireless exploits and countermeasures.